FORAIN

The Painter

H

Frontispiece LE CLIENT *or* MAISON CLOSE
1878. $9\frac{3}{4} \times 12\frac{3}{4}$ in.

FORAIN

The Painter

1852-1931

Lillian Browse

Paul Elek London

For S.H.L.

Published in Great Britain 1978 by
Elek Books Limited
54-58 Caledonian Road, London N1 9RN

ISBN 0 236 40097 5

Set in 12-14pt Garamond by Ronset Ltd. Darwen, Lancs. and
Printed in Great Britain:
Text by Unwin Brothers Limited, Old Woking, Surrey
Plates by Cheney & Sons Limited, Banbury, Oxon.

CONTENTS

ACKNOWLEDGEMENTS

No book of this kind can possibly be achieved without the active help and goodwill of many people in the world of museums, of the art trade and also of private owners. I have been fortunate enough to receive both in full measure and my gratitude goes to those mentioned individually as well as those who wish to remain anonymous. I also thank these often very busy people for their patience in replying to my continuous queries, despite which there is still so much that remains unanswered.

Beyond all, I am most grateful to Josef Herman who has encouraged me in whatever undertaking I have laid before him. His own impeccable literary gifts have rendered his suggestions invaluable; he has also made sure that I have committed no painterly gaffs and he has checked my translations. My dear friend, Mlle Nicole Villa of the Bibliothèque Nationale has, despite her own very active life, found time to help me once again and through her I have had great help from my researcher, Mlle Hélène Gaudin.

In Paris I have also to thank M. Jean Adhémar and M. Prinet, both of the Bibliothèque Nationale, M. Jean Lapeyre of the Louvre, M. Phillipe Reichenbach, M. Gruet of Bernheim-Jeune, Mme Huguette Beres, M. Yves St Laurent, and M. Charles Durand-Ruel who so generously opens the Durand-Ruel Archives to any who may need to consult them. In Copenhagen I especially thank Merete Bodelsen, the art historian.

In London Mr Jack Baer of the Hazlitt, Gooden & Fox Galleries has unfailingly done the many things I have asked of him, and I acknowledge with gratitude the various kindnesses of Mr Johns of Knoedler & Co., the Directors of the Reid Gallery and those of Arthur Tooth and Sons, Mr Julian Barron of Sotheby's, the librarians at Colnaghi & Co. and at the *Burlington Magazine*, Mr Antony Brett-James, Mr Nicholas Stewart and finally of Miss Edwina Sassoon, Miss Léna Holland and Miss Jean Berry— theirs for secretarial work.

I also had much pleasure in meeting the artist's granddaughter and her husband, M. and Mme Chagnaud-Forain. They received me with much hospitality and showed me over Forain's last home.

My one regret is that Paul Elek, who greeted this specialised book with warm enthusiasm, was not able to see it brought to fruition; my pleasure is that I have worked most happily with Miss Moira Johnston in whose hands I have been fortunate enough to find myself.

The author and publishers would like to thank S.P.A.D.E.M. and all those who gave permission for the reproduction of works in their possession.

FORAIN

1852-1931

'Have you read the latest Forain?'

This was a familiar morning greeting among Frenchmen who lived through the thirty-five years or so of Forain's brilliantly successful career as a cartoonist. His satirical comments in the daily and weekly papers were awaited with feverish excitement by Parisians and provincials alike.[1] These drawings together with their *légendes* formed a biting and highly personal entity. Léandre Vaillat had much to say about them in his book *En Ecoutant Forain* published in 1931, the year of the artist's death. The title gives the key not only to his own volume but also to the other two monographs and most of the numerous articles written on the cartoonist during and after his life. Forain's authors have laid particular stress upon his celebrated *bons mots* to the exclusion of much that would have been of greater value. It is true to say that he did come to exploit his wit socially until, like an actor who forgets how to be himself, the assumed personality became part of him. Whistler and Wilde were also of this ilk, but although writers made much of their witticisms, it was not to the neglect of their real work as was the case with Forain. The purpose of this book, therefore, is to try to present Forain, the draughtsman-painter, and deliberately to ignore the sardonic cracks with which his name has become irrevocably linked.

It is difficult nowadays to realise what tremendous power the satirical draughtsman once exercised upon the man-in-the-street. The influential political and social cartoonist no longer exists; gone are the days when his drawings comprised a compelling feature in nearly every paper. In Forain's time it was not at all unusual for him to be allotted as much as half a page or no less than a spread of six columns; on occasion he was even given the entire front page in colour. At the turn of the century there existed in France alone a whole body of gifted draughtsmen-satirists, among them Steinlen, Sem, Caran d'Ache and Willette. Forain is generally accepted as being the most important of all, even the greatest cartoonist since Goya and Daumier. This is probably a just assessment but it should not be assumed that, talented

9

though he was, Forain ever reached the heights of pure draughtsmanship attained by these two great masters. He was of a lesser calibre, but in his own scale marvellously well equipped. He had the capacity for prodigious work and was never satisfied until his drawings exactly expressed what he was determined to say, and in the most economical terms. Through fierce self-discipline his observation became deeply penetrating and his memory so firm that later he did not find it necessary to make sketches in the court-rooms for use in his paintings on that subject. His *légendes* were evidently as important as the drawings themselves, but it is well nigh impossible for a foreigner to judge the subtlety of their nuances, and the finer points of their topical content may be fully sensed only by a native. Edmond de Goncourt wrote: 'Ce Forain a une langue toute Parisienne, faite de ces expressions intraduisable dans une idiome quel'conque, et qui renferment le sublime d'une ironie infiniment délicate.'[2] Humour is one of those traits which, perhaps more than any other, defies the breaking down of national barriers; its roots lie too deeply embedded in centuries of history and racial characteristics for them to be penetrated by any *étranger*. Partisanship is another necessary component in the equipping of a cartoonist, but Forain went a step further. He prided himself upon being an inflexible character. Once he had decided upon who and what was right, who and what was wrong, nothing could alter him. He confused rigidity with strength. There are, however, instances in his private life that reveal another and more sympathetic side to his nature, when he is known to have performed kindly acts to help those who had offended him and were therefore classed as enemies. These 'weaknesses' had to be performed under the strictest secrecy, for he was clearly ashamed of them. Only his wife knew and sometimes betrayed her husband in order to disprove his reputation for heartlessness. In his family life Forain was a devoted, if difficult, husband and an adoring father who, though sometimes disappointed in his son, always forgave him his failings. Professionally he was full of prejudices, said by Degas to be the 'force of a society',[3] and one of the characteristics shared by Forain with that great genius was his overwhelming and epoch-defying anti-Semitism. Forain went so far as to refuse to believe in Captain Dreyfus' innocence even when, after those long years of tortuous exile, Dreyfus was at last proved the innocent victim of a perfidious plot. Not until after the 1914–18 war and when age had softened him, did Forain grudgingly admit that France's Jewish soldiers had also fought gallantly against the common foe. There are those who claim that his attitude over the *Affaire* was not that of an anti-Semite, but of a true patriot who could not accept the possibility of any such ignominy among the 'officers and gentlemen' of France; he believed, as Friedrich Sieburg so aptly put it, that God, without any doubt, is French. But Forain himself, recalling his fondness for Porto-Riche, a Jewish friend of his youth, is reported to have said: 'A cet âge-là, on ne faisait pas attention si un homme était Juif ou non. L'antisémitisme, c'est une chose qu'on découvre ensuite.'[4] Be that as it may, there is no escaping the fact that the man who fostered so many just causes through his pen and pencil could or would not recognise justice when it was on 'the other side of the fence'.

Forain, ironically, reached his heights as a draughtsman when he was being least admirable as a human being. A paradoxical and bewildering personality, the artist in him seemed to expand as the man with balanced judgement diminished. Perhaps it was this very hatred and fury that unleashed in the anti-Dreyfus drawings of 1898–9 certain inhibitions, a kind of smallness, still visible in those of the *Album Forain* of 1896 and of *Doux Pays* of the same year. 'Forain se couchait dans un état de rage, et se levait après un sommeil agité, plus en rage, ne voulant pas approfondir les côtes juridiques du procès, résolu à ne pas en discuter.'[5] The drawings in *Psst. . .!* revealed Forain as a fully equipped draughtsman. The expressiveness with which he handled the human body was complete; no longer could his figures be criticised as marionettes, they were people of flesh and blood. His compositions had become sure and interesting and the handling of the crayon masterly. The various borrowings had been absorbed and translated into entirely personal terms. These drawings are true Forain and while their sponsorship of gross injustice seems inexcusable in an artist who declared '. . . pour le bien de tous, je dénounce',[6] it is the aesthetic and not the moral issue which, here, is of primary importance.

It is very understandable that Forain's illustriousness as a satirist should have detracted from Forain the painter. These two professions are somewhat uncomfortable bedfellows and it cannot be denied that, by and large, Forain's least successful paintings suffer from this liaison in that their literary content is over-emphasised. Perhaps a second reason for his being neglected in this sense is that his pictures are mainly divided into two categories—up to the last decade of the century, the scenes of *La Vie Parisienne*, and after a gradual transition, the long series of Court-Rooms which continued until the end of his life. The formal approach of the latter bears little or no relation to that of the former, indeed each might have been achieved by a different hand. As nothing flatters the amateur's ego more than to be able to recognise a painter at a glance, this sharp diversity in Forain's work did not prove endearing. Furthermore, having started as a 'modern' in company with the Impressionists—than whom he was born about half a generation later as were Seurat, Van Gogh, Gauguin and Lautrec—he turned his back on the *Indépendants,* ignored the dawning of the twentieth century and the new languages of Modern Art, and deliberately took a retrogressive step towards Hals, Goya, and Daumier. Such a move was not likely to win the approval of subsequent historians.

Forain's own explanation of his volte-face was that his early training under Carpeaux eventually made him dissatisfied with the ideals of Impressionism: 'Les Impressionistes ont découvert le procédé pour peindre la lumière, trouvaille magnifique! Mais la nuage est splendide lui aussi. Sont splendides tous les tons de la grisaille.'[7] But whether Forain realised it or not this declaration had meaningful undertones. It was not only against the Impressionists' effects of light that he turned but also against their enchanting enjoyment of nature and simple every-day pleasures which even their own material hardships could not quell. It is exactly this aspect, of what would nowadays be called 'escapism', that has made Renoir, Pissarro, Monet, and Sisley so appealing to the general public. Forain may well have come to prefer the beauty of the *grisaille* and to have eschewed the colours born of the play of sunlight, but the underlying cause lay within the man who had moved away from the early delightful paintings of cafés and courtesans into a deeper concern for the human situation which, from the beginning, had peeped through most of his cartoons.

On 23 October 1852 a son named Jean-Louis was born to Charles Forain and his wife in the historic city of Rheims, the ancient town named after Saint Remi who had baptised Clovis—'le nouveau Constantin'—there in the year 496. The father was a house-painter but evidently a skilled artisan as well who specialised in the imitation of marble, oak and granite. In the days when individual workmanship was a cause for great pride and it was customary for a son to follow in his father's calling, when parents had fewer pretensions for the future of their children and certainly fewer possibilities for their fulfilment, Forain *père* hoped his son would presently join him in his trade. Somewhere around 1860 the family moved to Paris, and Jean-

Louis later said that he ran away from his new home in the following year, back to his grandparents in Rheims, and that the police were sent to fetch him.[8] How such an escapade was accomplished by a nine-year-old has never been revealed. Charles Forain must have had some feeling for the arts and inclinations beyond his normal work, for 'Au tableau-noir, il faisait des merveilles avec la craie',[9] and he also made a hobby of framing engravings. These hung on the walls of the family home and his son always felt that it was through them that he came to learn something about the history of France. Jean-Louis had one uncle who owned a mill at Bezannes on the mountain of Rheims; another was a grocer in a street leading to the great Cathedral, the setting for Charles VII's crowning—the culmination of Joan of Arc's triumph. Throughout his life Forain cherished the memory of this beautiful edifice and recalled that it was '. . . devant le Cathédral que j'ai vu dessiner pour la première fois'.[10] Like most other children he was given a box of crayons to help pass the time whenever he was ill and from these days of his childhood he knew, without a doubt, that he would become an artist.

Jean-Louis took his first Communion in Paris where the family home was in the rue de l'Université and he attended the local school. By his own account he was an inattentive and disinterested pupil who only wanted to draw and paint. As he had no pocket-money of his own, one of his schoolchums, Albert Bésnard, gave him chalks and crayons. Albert's parents were artists themselves. His father had been a pupil of Ingres and his mother was a miniaturist and, luckily for Jean-Louis, they were quite well-to-do. By the time Forain was fourteen he had become a regular visitor to the Louvre and here, away from the eyes of the attendants in the main galleries, he copied drawings, chiefly those of the great Primitive painters. One has become so accustomed to hearing this repetitious story about the beginnings of many a famous artist that it no longer seems to have much meaning. Yet it is not unremarkable that a country-bred youth should have been so drawn towards quality when he might easily have preferred works of more superficial attraction.

In the Louvre came the meeting with M. Jacquesson de la Chevreuse whose main claim to fame seems to be that he quickly recognised Jean-Louis' potential and that he did something about it. A painter of historical pictures in the manner of Paul Delaroche, his beautiful-sounding name is a far cry from that of his ancestor, an English squire called Jackson, who left the country of his birth in order to follow James II to France. One day when it was raining hard, M. Jacquesson de la Chevreuse, who had noticed Forain in the museum, offered to share his umbrella with the lad as they both happened to be leaving at the same moment. Jean-Louis confessed that he wanted to become an artist but that as it was against his family's wishes, he really did not know what to do. The older man was intrigued; he went home with the boy, examined his drawings, and persuaded the parents to allow him to instruct their son in 'les principes de mon art'. For nearly a year Jean-Louis worked in his studio. He was forbidden to draw upon tinted paper or to heighten any drawing with white. 'Plus tard, plus tard, quand tu peindras . . .'[11] he was told. Each morning early the artist, with Jean-Louis at his side, could be seen walking—a bus ride was never allowed—to hear Mass in one or other of Paris' forty basilicas, for being a man of great faith M. Jacquesson de la Chevreuse solicited the aid of the Almighty before he would begin his day's work. However, the time came when the kind but strict disciplinarian was so mortified by his pupil's behaviour that he made some family concern a reason for parting. He had always implored Jean-Louis to hold on to his faith and to avoid all bad company but when the latter confided this to his student pals, they teased the life out of him and from sheer devilry dragged him off to places of whose existence the innocent had not even been aware. This got to the master's ears and heralded the end of their relationship.

His parents now allowed Forain to become a student at the Ecole des Beaux-Arts where his friend Albert was already installed. Mme Bésnard's home was in the place Furstenberg, in that delightful house where Delacroix had lived, worked and died. Now the Musée Delacroix, it is a place of pilgrimage for the world-wide admirers of the great Romantic painter and although only poor reminders of his art hang on its walls, it is nevertheless impossible not to feel its unique atmosphere or a sense of privilege at being allowed to 'intrude'. Because of his friend, Forain was a frequent visitor and he was enchanted.

But again the same old story of an independent young spirit being unable to accept the dryness of school classes, the dreariness of drawing from a model calcified into some traditional pose, or the boredom of studying a neo-Antique plaster that was dead from top to toe. Away went Jean-Louis from the Ecole des Beaux-Arts back to his copying in the Louvre. Many people find that they have a way of drawing similar experiences to themselves because their subconscious feels the need and therefore places them in a state of receptiveness. So once again Forain was noticed in the gallery, this time as he was working on a head of a Satyr which he had planned to give his mother as a present. Suddenly he turned to find a small man with a big moustache and an Imperiale watching him. 'Ce n'est pas mal . . . pas mal du tout . . . il-y-a bien quelques erreurs . . . Attends!'—and with that he took the crayon and made certain incisive strokes of correction. Momentarily Jean-Louis was upset that the stranger should have spoilt his drawing but he quickly saw and admitted how very right these corrections were. A card was then thrust into his hand with the instructions: 'Viens me voir à l'atelier, un de ces matins.' Whether the name on the card meant anything to him or not he was soon to be enlightened by his amazed friends to whom he reported the incident. Carpeaux, they said, was a very famous sculptor, he was even 'le professeur de dessin du Prince Impérial' and Forain didn't know what a lucky chap he was! The very next morning Jean-Louis rushed off to the address given him in the faubourg St Honoré, a street then full of artists' studios and where he himself was to live not so many years hence. On the ground floor an elderly man was cutting into a vast marble figure, a student was modelling a bust. Carpeaux did not confine himself only to sculpture and upstairs was his painting atelier. Forain was disappointed to find the master was out but on seeing the pupil moulding the clay, his own fingers itched to do the same and he cheekily started to model a bas-relief. When it was time to leave Carpeaux had still not returned and Jean-Louis, obviously proud of his work, inscribed it with his own name and address. Then he waited hopefully. Some days later came a letter inviting him to visit the studio again. The sculptor greeted him—'Sais-tu qu'il est épatant ton bas-relief? . . . Seulement, il te faudra trente ans pour refaire ça. C'est très bien deviner; en attendant, il faut apprendre.'[12]

Carpeaux was then working on his most famous sculpture, *la Danse*, which although considered scandalous by traditionalists, was finally placed outside the Nouvel Opéra of Charles Garnier. He had been a pupil of François Rude, one of the many excellent and now neglected French sculptors of the first half of the nineteenth century. Rude was responsible for one of the bas-reliefs that adorn the Arc de Triomphe de l'Etoile but whose merits defy close appreciation on account of the great height at which they have been placed. In later years Forain liked to tell how each time he passed the Arc de Triomphe, Carpeaux would raise his hat in homage to his former teacher. Jean-Louis studied with Carpeaux for about a year, during which he was again allowed to try his hand at a bas-relief. The subject he chose was after an engraving which contained the figure of a blind man: 'Monsieur, je ne peux pas'.[13] Carpeaux smiled, and told his pupil to go out into the street, look for a blind man under some doorway, and then return and try again. This was Forain's first lesson in the observation of life around him, the observation that was to comprise the very structure of his art. During his year with Carpeaux he was taught the elements of sculpture, but the master obviously began to realise that his pupil's talents had little affinity with this particular branch of art so he sent the young man to work also with the painter Dumont. A few examples of Forain's efforts at sculpture exist but they are more remarkable for their historic interest than for their artistic merit.

Jean-Louis soon discovered the treasure-house that is the Cabinet des Estampes in the Bibliothèque Nationale; today its wonderful collection includes more than 2500 of his drawings for journals. Here, and without any particular plan, he continued to copy the *chefs-d'oeuvre* of the great masters, especially those of Holbein, whose wonder for him was 'La resemblance rigoureuse des traits dans les visages'.[14] But one evening while walking through the Cabinet he suddenly noticed an album of Goya's most beautiful prints upon a table. Forain was transfixed. This was just what he wanted to be able to do. Straightaway he went out into the street, bought a notebook and without seeking any particular figure, as he had done with his blind man, he sketched as swiftly as possible anyone who came his way. As may be seen he had become a truly assiduous worker, dividing his time between the studios of Carpeaux and Dumont, the museums, the libraries and above all the pavements of Paris on which were to be found a mingling of happiness and tragedy, wealth and poverty, drabness and excitement. Still in his teens, he was well on the way to equipping himself for the exciting rôle of the artist whose *métier* is far more demanding, far more difficult than the outside world can ever realise.

Carpeaux was by all accounts a heavy drinker and therefore was not always in the best of humours. One morning, after a 'heavy night', he turned his pupil out, according to Jean-Louis, for a mere trifle. Forain *père* was also enraged with his son, whose crime would seem to have been more serious than he cared to confess—'Mon père me maudit, ou à peu près, et me voilà sur le pavé de Paris.'[15] What actually happened nobody seems to have known; the event became embedded in silence just as later did the long breach in Forain's friendship with Huysmans. Neither has any light been thrown upon the duration of the rupture with his parents, but a reunion must have taken place within the next two or three years, for around 1872 Forain painted a tiny portrait of his mother which hung over his bed until the day of his death. But now he was on his own, without a home, without money and never having earned a sou in his life. He was approaching eighteen and it was 1870, that fateful year in the history of France. He slept where he might, under bridges and in doorways, hungry and frightened though *un brave* as he was.[16] Then André Gill took him in, taught him painting and befriended him, as subsequently he was to help the youthful Rimbaud found asleep one day in Gill's unlocked room. A rabbit was painted on the door of Gill's studio in Montmartre which became famous as the Lapin à Gill when afterwards it was turned into a café, of its kind the best known in Paris. It was visited by countless tourists to the city who seemed enormously to enjoy the smoke-filled and incredibly noisy atmosphere of *La Vie Bohème* as they imagined it to have been in the late nineteenth century. The kindly André Gill went mad some ten years later, and sadly enough his fame rests more upon the café which bore his name than upon his own gifts as an artist and qualities as a human being.

With the war of 1870, the Parisians braced themselves for those long nineteen weeks of siege, alternating between hope and despair according to fatuous official reports or dishonest propaganda and their own innate common sense. Those who had the means left the capital while there was still the opportunity to do so, for soon all exits were blocked, balloons became the only method of transport with their limited accommodation reserved for a few courageous officials, and carrier-pigeons the single link with the world outside. Forain joined a battalion of engineers and earned thirty sous a day; he fought fires and carried sandbags through the tunnel to the fort of Montrouge—'On entendait les projectiles venant de Saint-Cloud, de Bellevue. Cela faisait comme des éclairs de chaleur à l'horizon.'[17]

A youth named Arthur Rimbaud escaped from his home in Charleville soon after peace had been declared. His mother had hoped that this gifted but impossible son of hers would return to the reopened school, as had his friends, but even boys of Arthur's age were affected by the general spirit of revolt that was smouldering until, a few months later, it suddenly burst into the horrors that were the Commune of Paris. Apart from this, Arthur had long been sulking in rebellion against authority and especially against the almost pathological discipline enforced upon him by his mother. Throughout his boyhood it had plagued and thwarted him. Whenever Arthur could escape the maternal eye he and his schoolfriend, Delahaye, would meet in the fields to discuss literature, politics and revolutionary ideas. Although buried in the country they both knew of the uprising by the Republicans of Paris against re-elected Royalists and 'right-wingers'; of the hoards who were marching into the capital, not only of Frenchmen but of all nationalities—'the vultures of every revolution'. This was Arthur's chance; he too would go to Paris. He walked all the way, but after days of wandering about trying to find work and having undergone some unknown, but shocking, experience he walked back again to his hated home, arriving like a frightened rabbit. At seventeen, Rimbaud still looked like a child, and a pretty girl at that, so it is not difficult to envisage what sort of experience he had suffered.

At school he had included Verlaine among his heroes, had won prizes declaiming the older man's poetry and had been influenced by him in the writing of his own precocious and beautiful verse. Verlaine, whose life was to be shattered by alcoholism and eventually by the irresistible attraction which the young Rimbaud held for him, was, in the autumn of 1871, married and respectably living with his wife's parents. The dissolute poet was just balancing upon the edge of a cliff, but for the moment all was well. Then came a letter of self-introduction from Rimbaud, and in the same envelope the boy had enclosed a few of his own verses as an added reference. Struck by both their quality and their originality Verlaine sent his fatal reply: 'Venez, chère grande âme, on vous attend, on vous désire.'[18] For the second time Rimbaud escaped to Paris, but on this occasion he sold his watch to pay for the journey. This was the beginning of the tumultuous and passionate relationship between the two poets. Rimbaud spent a few days, intolerable on both sides, with the Verlaine *ménage*, then he fled. Verlaine, understandably anxious about his welfare and feeling responsible for Arthur's being in Paris, took him temporarily to André Gill and finally to his own unfurnished attic which he kept as his place of work. But nowhere could Rimbaud settle, nowhere was he allowed to stay. His habits were too unspeakable and his way of life already too debauched—'There is a most alarming poet, not yet eighteen ... exhibited by Paul Verlaine his inventor. ... Such is the boy, whose imagination is a compound of great power and undreamt corruption.'[19]

The literary lunches of the *Vilains Bonshommes* were held periodically at the Café du Théâtre Bobino and attended by many of the foremost writers of the day. Forain was allowed to join them in exchange for which privilege he made drawings on the Café walls. It was probably here that he first met Verlaine and Rimbaud—the latter was soon to be banned on account of his offensive behaviour. Forain drew a head of Rimbaud at this time which appeared opposite the title page of *Les Mains de Jeanne Marie,* published posthumously in 1919. The poem was written at Charleville in 1871 when Rimbaud was sixteen; in the drawing he looks just like a very young child, while the hand is not at all recognisable as that of Forain.

A curious friendship was struck between these three. Forain evidently became genuinely fond of the pair of brilliant, licentious poets, for thirteen years later, in 1884, he wrote to Verlaine arranging a reunion and recalling affectionately the days when the two of them, with Rimbaud, would meet— 'C'est sans doute samedi dans la soirée que je voudrais te serrer la main et causer avec toi. . . . Où est le temps où nous t'attendions, Rimbaud et moi, dans un petit café de la rue Drouot, en fumant des pipes en terre que nous humections avec de nombreux bitter-curaço, il y a treize ans!'[20] The use of the pronoun *tu* shows how intimate was their relationship. Verlaine's attic was in the rue Campagne-Première and as Forain was homeless at the time of their meeting he was only too happy, for a while at least, to share it with Rimbaud— 'J'ai logé deux mois avec lui . . . dans un taudis épouvantable; ça lui convenait, ça lui plaisait, il était si sale. Nous avions qu'un lit, lui couchait sur les ressorts et moi par terre sur le matelas. . . . La vie avec Rimbaud n'était pas possible, parce qu'il buvait de l'abstinthe et de formidable façon. Verlaine venait le chercher et tous deux me méprisaient parce que je ne les suivais pas. Ce fut là tout leur vice. On a parlé de rapports antisexuels. Ah! non, je n'ai jamais rien vu, je n'y crois pas du tout. . .'.[21] But nobody ever knew what Forain really thought about the 'unnatural' relationship that undoubtedly existed between the two poets, for M. Gimpel's account is in direct contradiction to that of M. Puget. On this particular subject he was only able to extract one slight reference from Forain, who admitted that he had told Verlaine ' ". . . le genre de tes amours me dégoute. . . . Tu me parles d'idéal, de communion d'esprit: . . ." (Et, ici, un mot irrépétable)'.[22] Verlaine told his wife: 'Quand je suis avec la petite chatte brune [Forain], je suis bon car la petite chatte brune est très douce. Quand je suis avec la petite chatte blonde [Rimbaud], je suis mauvais, car la petite chatte blonde est féroce'.[23] Professionally *la petite chatte brune* was to become extremely *féroce* himself and as to any gentleness, this was to be reserved for his family and perhaps for a few friends.

After Verlaine, in a drunken fury, had almost killed his child and tried to strangle his wife, she agreed to forgive and return to him on the condition that Rimbaud be sent back to Charleville and that all association between the two should definitely come to an end. The remorseful and frightened husband agreed and, for the second time, Rimbaud returned to his home. But so obsessed was Verlaine that he could not bear the separation and lack of news, so illicit letters passed to and fro, with Forain acting as the forwarding agent. Although disgusted with the pair, he continued as a faithful friend and in June 1872 he wrote telling Rimbaud that he hoped soon to have a studio of his own and asking him quickly to send his news.

In 1873 Forain was sleeping in a shed in the rue Monsieur le Prince which he shared with several comrades. One night an unknown man came into the 'dormitory', announced himself as being the proprietor of Au Petit Tambour, and said that he wanted to change its sign. He had been advised to call on Forain! With the greatest possible surprise and joy Forain undertook the task, not only his first commission but his very first sale. Perhaps, by this time, he was receiving a little help from his parents although there are no known records to affirm this surmise. In any case, in the spring of that year, his living problems were temporarily solved for he was called up to do military service and went to Laval to join a regiment of infantry.

Forain started his first four professional years, not as a cartoonist but as a painter and etcher. His early tentative pictures were mainly in watercolour for the simple reason that he seldom had the money with which to buy oil-paint and canvas. Where and how he came to meet Degas does not seem to have been told. What is certain is that this meeting with its subsequent effects turned out to be of the greatest importance in the young man's career and even in his life, for Degas was to become his professional mentor and life-long friend. It is well known that Degas had a very restricted circle of friends whom, as he was far from being gregarious, he chose with the utmost care and who mostly did not happen to be painters. To have been included among the elect was an enormous privilege and one that carried much weight especially for a young artist trying to make a start. Through Degas, Forain was introduced to the painters and writers who had formerly gathered at the Café Guerbois and were now moving to the Nouvelle Athènes. Among this group was Manet.

The Realist movement, which had started in the field of literature with the novels of Balzac, was taken up by Courbet when, in 1849, he painted his enormous canvas *Un Enterrement à Ornans*—a picture that is a landmark in the history of art, later to be equalled in importance by, for instance, Picasso's *Les Demoiselles d'Avignon*. After six years Courbet produced his second huge Realist painting, *l'Atelier du Peintre*, upon whose heels followed the earliest of Daumier's series, *Un Wagon de Troisième Classe*. Manet extended and developed this vein of Realism which he and others moulded in their various ways in agreement with Impressionist tenets. For a short while Manet had begun by paying tribute to the Spanish school but immediately after, at the age of thirty, he evolved his personal method which became known as *peinture claire*. Thus he became the first of the Impressionist painters who, once the 'shock' had passed, gradually began to be appreciated, until finally Impressionism enjoyed fantastic acclaim—an acclaim that has only abated during the last few years.

The Impressionists were Realists in that they favoured the every-day life scene whether it consisted of people, landscape or a combination of both. They differed from the movement in so far as they laid more stress upon the accidental, saw the half of life as being happy rather than the half of life as being sad—which attitude greatly contributed to the subsequent popularity of their work—and were absorbed by a completely new interest—the behaviour of sunlight upon any given scene and the colours in its resultant shadows. Whether or not they had remained in Paris during the Siege and the Commune, the Impressionists had not felt the necessity for painting the horrors of those days. Neither Manet nor Degas—the latter was never a true Impressionist—was fascinated by natural landscape; they expressed themselves through the human form, a choice which Forain was to prove he shared. It is not surprising, therefore, that these two painters were to have the greatest effect upon his early pictures, for Forain was already conditioned to the observation of the life around him. The idea had been installed by Carpeaux and reinforced by his discovery of Goya's prints—two disparate influences, with the study of man as the common denominator.

The earliest known paintings by Forain date from about 1872—*Portrait de la Mère de l'Artiste*, already mentioned, and *Au Café*, a watercolour of the same date which, in vision, closely resembles the artist's first attempts at etching. He also painted a few still life canvases such as *Bouquet de Violettes*, never completed through lack of paints, and *Bouteille de Marasquin avec un Paquet de Biscuits* which he submitted to the Salon of 1874. Degas, anyhow, strongly disapproved of this gesture and was said to have been highly delighted at its refusal by the jury. Most of Forain's paintings around the middle seventies, though seen through the eyes of Manet yet sometimes wearing the pince-nez of Degas, were glazed with an undeniably amusing irony which foreshadowed the cartoonist he was to become. His first satirical drawing was accepted by *le Scapin* in the spring of 1876, an inferior drawing with an inferior *légende,* but it represented his first professional acceptance. The name of Forain had appeared in print. In the winter of the same year another was published by *la Cravache*, this one so adept, so telling, that thirteen years later Huysmans still remembered it in *la Revue Illustrée*: '. . . c'était une terrible et vrai merveille'.[24] Also in 1876, Forain wrote to Huysmans: 'J'ai à faire pour *la République des lettres* des dessins. J'ai besoin d'un texte. Trouvez-moi donc quelques poèmes en prose. Des choses parisiennes bien entendu. . . . Avec votre cruelle ça irait très bien. . . .'[25] Commissions from this and that journal came slowly trickling in; these drawings were all on social themes and it was not until the summer of 1880 that one of Forain's first political cartoons appeared, in the Royalist paper *le Monde Parisien.*

For various reasons Renoir, Sisley, Berthe Morisot and Cézanne had all decided not to participate in the fourth Impressionist Exhibition of 1879, a serious loss indeed. Degas, still one of the leaders of the movement, knew it was necessary to reinforce the number of exhibitors and took this opportunity of introducing the work of Forain and another disciple-friend, Mary Cassatt. Forain showed one portrait in oils and twenty-five *aquarelles* which included more portraits, scenes in cafés and theatres, and a number of fans— then much in vogue. Huysmans, whose articles on the Salon of that year were to establish him as a foremost art-critic, wrote of it: '. . . Ici rien; les Indépendants sont décidément les seuls qui puissent rendre ou essayent au moins de rendre la Parisienne et la fille. Il y a plus d'élégance, plus modernité dans le moindre ébauche de femme de L. Forain que dans toutes les toiles des Bouveret et autre fabricants de faux monde! . . . ce sont de petites merveilles de la réalité parisienne et élégante.'[26]

When Huysmans wrote this he was thirty-one and had already spent thirteen years as a minor official in the Ministry of the Interior. He was slightly older than Forain and the two had been friends since 1876 at least. Both men looked through the window of satire on to the situation of man-kind, the writer and artist each expressing himself with particular individuality through the means of his chosen *métier*. In 1876 Huysmans had stolen a march on Edmond de Goncourt by getting his *Marthe* published just ahead of de Goncourt's *La Fille Elisa,* thus making it the first French novel on the life of a licensed prostitute. Forain had done an etching as a frontispiece which now appears to us as enchantingly witty. It shows 'Marthe' standing and holding an umbrella but clad only in striped stockings. Hoping to get the book past the French customs by making it appear as harmless as possible, the Brussels publishers had—uselessly as it turned out—refrained from using any illustrations. This particular etching of Forain's (Plate i) was never published. For the second, and French, edition of 1879 he did another, a much less interesting plate. The censors had pulled the reins too tightly and, not having been given a free head, Forain's second attempt was weak and self-conscious but, at least, it was accepted.

Like Baudelaire before him, Huysmans was one of those singular literary men who had a feeling for the pictorial arts and whose discerning, fearless judgement made him into a prophetic art critic. Among the first to recognise the revolution brought about by the Impressionists, he was delighted not only with the method of painting they had evolved but equally with the choice of the contemporary scene as their subject. This was the attitude of de Goncourt, Huysmans' hero, and of the great Naturalist writers. Huysmans considered Forain the supreme painter of the prostitute, hence the *Marthe* commission. The writer accumulated a small collection of works by Degas, Cézanne, Guys, Raffaëlli, Rops, and among them, occupying 'a place of honour',[27] was a pastel portrait that Forain made of him about 1878 (Plate 3).

Forain continued to exhibit with the Impressionists for the following two years as well as in their final exhibition of 1886. Regardless of Degas, he also submitted pictures to the Salon. The subjects of his first period comprised cafés, Folies, brothels, *femmes d'élégance, coulisses de l'Opéra*, portraits of friends and a small number of people in landscapes. Not an original list but in keeping with his time.

In contrast with his social cartoons, these pictures are almost entirely the output of a painter commenting upon and enjoying a particular side of the Paris scene, with nearly always a little snigger behind the humour. Outwardly their mood is the essence of frivolity but the frivolity is merely a mask. Nothing could appear gayer than the *cocotte* in *La Rencontre au Foyer* (Plate I) with her pert little face and sham innocent eyes, surrounded by top-hatted gentlemen whose hopes are very evident; or *Le Client* (frontispiece), a title acceptable in the days of 'naughty' Paris but which, when mythology was *à la mode*, might well have been called *The Judgement of Paris*. Before the client parades a bevy of well-fed nudes, again in striped stockings, and in feathered, exposing wraps with a crucifix pointedly hanging around the neck of one of them—a deliciously naughty picture. Both of these paintings reveal an already sophisticated sense of composition and a decorative choice of local colour. Another of this group is *Scène de Café* (Plate 2) which, although in conception recalling Manet's *Au Bar aux Folies Bergère*, is actually dated three years earlier than that famous picture was painted. In these works around 1878 it is interesting to note that Forain used a 'hatching' stroke with his brush, a method more usually employed in drawing.

Towards the eighties, Forain's young women with their tiny *retroussé* noses and round black spots for eyes, gradually changed from this particular recipe into women with some individuality. The artist had become beguiled by the mystery which a veil could impart to the most ordinary of faces and as this fashion was much in vogue, he repeatedly made use of it. In 1881, the Jardin de Paris succeeded Le Bal Musard as a favourite place of amusement, and there Forain painted at least three pictures two of which, (Plates 10 and 13) in their different ways, are reminiscent of Manet's *Musique aux Tuileries* of 1862. These, together with a few panels of women *se promenant au bord de la mer,* represent the first of Forain's rare out-of-doors paintings. Those of the Jardin de Paris can hardly, however, be said to embrace any landscape, for their illuminated trees and groups of dandies accompanied by lady friends hem in the leading characters as did the walls of the earlier brothels and cafés. Forain had already developed a remarkable ability to handle crowds and, through his penchant for artificial lighting, was able to infuse his canvases with a certain sense of excitement—*l'Acrobate* (Plate 7) is an excellent example of the combination of these two qualities. But without the firm underlying drawing any picture is a 'hit or miss' affair and Forain was eminently a draughtsman. He could, by now, do much as he wanted with the human figure; he was the master and the pencil was his tool. Everything that really matters is revealed through the weight, shape and stance of his bodies; not only are they aesthetically satisfying but also from the point of view of characterisation they indicate exactly what kinds of people are contained within their outward show. No details of ambiance are necessary, no facial expressions or clothes. There are 'gros messieurs paternels et obscènes',[28] servile waiters, and hopeless, abandoned girls. Forain was a story-teller in paint as were some of the greatest artists of his day. But it is one thing to work on a small scale and quite another on a large, and it then remained to be seen whether Forain would ever have the power to sustain, or the vision to conceive, full-size canvases.

René Princeteau, the painter of horses and dogs, was a friend of the

Toulouse-Lautrec family and an immediate neighbour of Forain's when, by 1884, the latter had been able to rent a studio in the faubourg Saint Honoré. Both Princeteau and le Comte de Toulouse-Lautrec included Forain among their circle of intimates. The Comte's crippled son was then studying with the deaf-mute Princeteau—a sadly incongruous pair; he was also taking lessons from another *animalier*, the French-born, but of Irish origin, John Lewis-Brown. Of his father's three artist friends, Lautrec drew more closely to the oncoming cartoonist. He admired the sharp and economic clarity of Forain's line drawings, the mocking wit and the caustic satire levelled against the strata of society that infuriated him. In retrospect it could not have been otherwise, and Lautrec's later work was not uninfluenced by this rebellious draughtsman by the side of whom he was, in the 1890s, a contributor to the same periodicals. Forain did a portrait drawing of the Comte which his son always kept as a treasured possession, and Lautrec is reported to have said, after he left his teachers to re-start away from the Naturalist tradition, 'I don't belong to any school. I work in my corner. I admire Degas and Forain.'[29]

Forain was still having a struggle to make ends meet: three more years were to pass before he would have a regular income and, in the meantime, life was precarious. Often hungry during the day, he somehow managed to buy a 'smoking' for the evenings when he was invited to smart dinner or theatre parties, for he was beginning to be taken up by society. The 'Gavroche' had come a long way from the days when he slept on the floor of Verlaine's attic, and he was flattered; besides, he could make use of his hosts as they of him. Both he and they had their particular brand of snobbism, as who has not? On their side his wit was of social value and they sensed that he might eventually become a celebrity. Forain, who found that the fashionable artists Helleu, Sargent and Tissot were also at these gatherings, encountered a side of life that hitherto he had only heard about but could not have dreamt that he would ever witness at firsthand. He painted a few Ballroom scenes—perhaps prompted by Tissot's *Too Early*—discussed further on, and later some highly satirical *Soirées Musicaux*. He also managed to sell a few small pictures to members of Parisian society whom he met on these occasions, thus earning some badly needed money. In an effort to make his mark in the Salon of 1884 he painted a rather large picture of a ball in progress, a *tour de force* as far as he was concerned for he had never before extended

himself to such a size. A well-controlled canvas carried to its final conclusion, *Le Buffet* (Plate 15) is an admirable painting in the academic idiom, but how sadly distant from the teachings of Manet and Degas. And yet what acute *rapportage*! One might have supposed it to have been painted as a result of a visit to London, for the young girls at the ball comport themselves in the manner that the French choose to regard as typical of the English 'Miss'—rigid as soldiers, cold and dignified, always mistresses of their emotions, that is if they have any. But obviously débutantes in French society of the eighties were no different from their counterparts across the Channel for one may be sure that Forain's portrayal was exact. As for the men, they are gallantly courteous if not politely disinterested; not a single base thought is allowed to escape from the polished minds of these well-bred gentlemen in the ambiance of the smart salons from where they will finally choose, not their mistresses, but their wives. Forain painted two other pictures of this genre, *Entreé dans le Monde* and a pastel *En Soirée*. In the Salon of 1885 he exhibited another largish picture, *Le Veuf* (Plate 16), in which a bourgeois, clad in black and wearing his top-hat, sits disconsolately in his wife's bedroom surrounded by her personal apparel. He is mourning the treasure he has lost, and if ever there was a picture with a thrusting message, this is it. It is very evident that Forain was still pandering to the jury and their taste for 'sob-stuff', for *Le Veuf* is sentimental in the extreme and cannot be redeemed by its good composition and sense of scale, some fine passages of paint together with charming areas of colour.

In the same year as *Le Buffet*, the bewildering Forain painted two delicious 'outsiders'—*Le Pêcheur* (Plate 19) and *Femme à sa Toilette* (Plate IV). Like *Le Veuf*, *Le Pêcheur* also represents a solitary, seated figure of a man, but in this instance Forain was not deliberately working for an exhibition but was allowing himself the freedom of painting a scene which certainly enchanted him and touched his sense of humour. What a world of difference there is between these two canvases and how illuminating is the comparison. *Le Pêcheur* shows a little fisherman seated somewhat precariously at the end of a plank, with his dog at his side. He is balanced over the water, in whose depths are reflected the bridge and the foliage on the far bank. No details of the surroundings are given but all is made known through suggestion achieved by the use of thin, rather liquid pigment, sensitive in the gradation of its tones in the manner of a Whistler. In contrast, the fisherman and his dog are precisely stated, but the whole has been solved in so painterly a fashion that the picture 'holds' beautifully together. Its air of whimsicality makes one chuckle for the sheer fun of it. *Femme à sa Toilette* is permeated with the same kind of quizzical humour. Its effects are obtained through similar means; in this case the figure, instead of being silhouetted, is completely fused into its surroundings. Being almost monochromatic, the weight of its masses depends equally upon its exact understanding of drawing and tonal values. Like the edges of the figure, the *objets de toilette*, though boldly stressed, also melt into the background and, in nice juxtaposition, are arranged as well-defined emphases in the lower part of the picture plane, thus completing a semi-circular flow which terminates with the head. The largeness of scale and simple triangular composition—which Forain was frequently to use in his later Court-Room scenes—are repeated in the delightful pastel on a related theme, *Femme se Regardant au Miroir* (Plate 22). Whereas this pastel is perhaps more easily recognisable than the canvas, both represent a facet less obviously familiar in Forain's *oeuvre*.

The first drawings by Jean-Louis Forain appeared in *le Courrier Français* in September 1887, the beginning of his regular contributions to any journal. In 1888 and again in 1890 he produced no less than one hundred drawings in each year for this paper alone. Forain was thirty-five and from then on, as a draughtsman-satirist, his output was enormous as his rise to fame was steep.

'Les nombreuses scènes comportant des danseuses qu'il donne d'abord à ce journal semblent un homage à son mâitre Degas.'[30] Since the early seventies the *rats de l'Opéra*, as well as the *sujets* and *étoiles*, had been used by Degas with brilliant objectivity. His only real interest was in their relationship with ballet, the art that presented such an eternity of possibilities to his particular aesthetic and formal ideals. Yet to the always poor little *rats*, Degas behaved with kindly courtesy as he requested them to pause for a moment while rushing along a corridor or up the Opera stairs. They became the subjects of his masterpieces in charcoal, pastel and paint. Ludovic Halévy, among the writers, published in 1883 a volume called *La Famille Cardinal* which was the combination of two small books he had written a few years earlier. This delightful story tells of the two small daughters of a little bourgeois family who had both been entered at the Opera as *rats*. To the pride of their parents both achieved success; one married an aristocrat, the other became a wealthy *mondaine*. Although written in the form of a novel with an exceptionally happy ending, *La Famille Cardinal* has a background of realism: the humble parents of these children habitually had longings more material than artistic when they sent their daughters into the world that was the Paris Opera House. In his drawings for *le Courrier Français*, Forain turned the subject of the dance to yet another use, that of social satire. It was not the ballet as such that made him linger in the Opera; he never acquired a passion for it as did Degas who more than likely was responsible for his going there in the first instance. In the last decades of the nineteenth century, the little *rats de l'Opéra* were the favourite and possibly the easiest prey of those young 'sparks' and licentious middle-aged men seeking an after-dinner sport. The pathetic plight of these young girls, the avarice of their mothers, the mean and heartless animal-greed of their 'admirers', were what Forain set out to flay. But just occasionally his comments were more muted and he turned his attention towards a higher stratum of society whose behaviour was, outwardly at least, more circumspect. For a short while the dancers attracted Forain almost to the exclusion of everything else, but during his career as a cartoonist he covered a very wide field and the list of his 'pet hates' is long. More and more the political scene began to occupy him and whereas his domestic satires had been sarcastic, his political drawings became positively vitriolic. Influential daily and weekly papers as well as illustrated magazines now competed for his services, but the full list of those with whom he worked is far too extensive to quote in detail.

It is not easy to keep pace with Forain's various activities during this time without turning his story into a boring catalogue. Besides being a cartoonist and a painter, he was also an assiduous print-maker who developed into one of very fine quality. He began etching in the early seventies, but actually made his début as an engraver in 1880 when he was the principal illustrator for Huysmans' *Croquis parisiens*. He continued etching for about another ten years then abandoned the plate and turned to lithography. In this medium he worked directly on to the stone, a practice that suited him excellently and coincided, as was logical, with the drawings he was then doing in rich, black chalk. In his approaching maturity as an artist, Forain found that these two methods gave him the possibilities of breadth and freedom that he then required, of greater impact and more spontaneity. The drawings culminated in the magnificent but terrible series which appeared on the covers of *Psst . . . !* of 1898–9 published by Forain himself. Inside were the ink drawings of Caran d'Ache, his equally vehement collaborator, and in a whole issue of eighty-five numbers these two men poured out their hatred of the Jewish race, which they, like so many of their compatriots, considered the prime enemy of France. The lithographs continued until about 1910 and include the splendid *Cabinets Particuliers* whose nudes are reminiscent of Degas; portraits of Colette (Plate iii), Renoir (Plate xxiii), and Vollard as well as at least two self-portraits. Like Sickert, Forain did many portraits of himself in varying mediums during the course of his life and the amusing yet valid reasons for the English painter's tendency, quoted by Osbert Sitwell: '. . . after all you can always paint yourself, it is cheaper and you are easier to find'[31], might well have applied to him excepting that the majority of Forain's self-portraits were done when money was no longer a problem. When she sat for her portrait Colette wrote that she had been intimidated by the young, bearded and laughing Forain and that she had dared to ask why he had drawn her with only one eye. The answer came: '. . . because you probably only had one eye on that day'. During the few sittings she gave him, Colette watched him drawing upon the stone, destroying several. His glances were sparkling, sharp and objective, and she resentfully noted that very young girls do not like to be treated as if they are no more than a still life.

Forain may be said to have stabilised his public image and his private life in the nineties. In 1890 he held his first one-man exhibition. This comprised only drawings and it took place in the galleries of Boussod-Valadon in Paris. By 1889 he had met the young girl who was to become his wife. In the summer of that year '. . . trouve à Florian le joyeux Forain tout en flanelle blanche. Il m'a présenté à sa jolie compagne . . .', for Mlle Bosc was also in Venice, where Forain had evidently followed her. He had already proposed, but she hesitated to bind herself and preferred simply to be his pupil. Mlle Jeanne Bosc was the daughter of an 'austere professor' and hardly twenty years old. 'Elle est si adorablement jolie que nous assistons au triomphe de sa beauté. . . . Les hommes la contemplent en silence et les femmes détaillent ses graces dans le doux langage vénitien. . . .'[32] But Forain was evidently persuasive and able to overcome Jeanne's fears, for in the following year they were engaged and in 1891 they married. It was a late marriage for Forain, who was already well into middle age by the time Jean-Loup, their only child, was born in 1895. Whatever escapades Forain might have got up to before he met with Jeanne, he seems to have remained a devoted and faithful husband and father with no breath of scandal ever having attended his doings after he became a married man. A prosaic, non-Bohemian story.

Unwittingly, the young Mlle Bosc had scored a triumph that very few others could ever have claimed. She had turned the tables on Forain and for once it was he who was to become the object of someone's mockery. It made him touchingly apprehensive. In 1890 he wrote to her regretting that they had been unable to pass a particular afternoon together. 'Je suis certain que cela ne vous a pas beaucoup privée, mais moi . . . je m'arrête parce que je vais vous écrire une lettre d'amour et vous êtes beaucoup trop moqueuse pour que j'ose me livrer . . .'[33] This independent and spirited girl, who had decided to wait a little before consenting to marry Forain, was an accomplished pastelliste who after their wedding had her own studio in the Forain *ménage*. Edmond de Goncourt met her seven months after the event at a dinner party: someone, he wrote, he was curious to see nearby. He described her as having a pointed nose, and clear eyes beneath a forest of blond hair the colour of hemp and piled up like a clown's wig. Very coaxing, and with a teasing note in her voice. He went on to say that she was about to give up painting for cooking for, among her other culinary triumphs, she made a *paté de fois en croute* like nobody else '. . . et une croute, s'il vous plait, ou elle peint des fleurs avec du jaune d'oeuf, et des feuilles avec je ne sais quoi: de la patisserie artistique'.[34] Another of Mme Forain's interests was in the sculpting and production of marionettes. In 1906 she organised, under the nom de plume of 'Mère Gigone', a theatre of marionettes which she called 'le Théâtre des Nabots'. She made all the figures herself, Jean-Loup helped in their manipulation, and Forain did a lithograph for the cover of the programme. Degas attended some of these performances which were held in aid of poor children.

At the age of sixty Mme Forain, in her great big velvet hat and long cloak, was still elegant, gay and pretty and so she always remained. She had learned how to live in serenity with her devoted—though far from easy—husband, and was an adept in the art of appearing submissive while quietly getting her own way in the end. An art, perhaps, particular to Frenchwomen.

Somewhere around the middle nineties, Forain received a second commission to decorate a café, but in very different circumstances from the Café du Théâtre Bobino 'commission' of 1871. In succession to many others, a new café was to be opened at the corner of the rue le Peletier and the Boulevard des Italiens. For months the curiosity of passers-by was aroused because the building was completely hidden by hoardings. 'On the eve of the opening all the papers proclaimed in chorus—for a consideration, needless to remark— the sumptuousness of the art decorations in the new establishment. At last, like the walls of Jericho, the boards fell asunder and revealed a truly horrid spectacle. Nothing more hideous was ever seen in this world. It was like a combination between a butcher's shop and a bathing establishment. . . . However, the architect—or architects—conceived one happy idea . . . M. Forain, the brilliant draughtsman . . . was invited to do some mosaic cartoons to serve as a frieze for the façade between the windows of the first story.'[35] Forain's mosaics—the only ones he appears ever to have designed—were pronounced charming and simple in their decorative scheme. Appropriately they comprised typical café scenes—single figures eyeing each other from adjoining tables, others in evening dress, conversing, and couples waltzing. The Café Riche, together with the building in which it was housed, was pulled down in 1922 to make way for the Boulevard Haussmann extension; this is a pity as it is very possible that its architecture would now be found as charming as then it was distasteful. The mosaics themselves have been dispersed but two, with their attendant cartoons, may be seen at the Musée des Arts Decoratifs, Paris, and two others at the Musée Municipal, Meudon.

In 1893 Forain won his first official recognition when he was made a Chevalier de la Légion d'Honneur and in the same year there took place, at the Galerie Georges Petit, a Vente de Dessins de Forain in which 140 drawings were included. He and Jeanne took another trip to Venice, where he made a minute sketch in oils of her in front of St Mark's. One might have imagined that Forain would have painted his attractive wife more frequently, but curiously enough I have only traced one painting that is definitely accepted as being a portrait of her (Plate 49). It is known that he made one other attempt but was so dissatisfied with it that he worked and reworked it until it was a complete wreck. But Forain, with his strict self-censorship, must have known that he was no natural portraitist. Despite the number he essayed, they never got further than the state of impressions, and often very unsatisfactory ones at that.

By the time their son was born the couple were living in an apartment on the boulevard Gouvion-Saint-Cyr from where, in the following year, they moved to 30 bis rue Spontini. Forain, by now a man of some substance, built himself a mansion at this address, where he lived and worked until the last years of his life. To feel himself permanently established must have been an enormous relief, and being a man of serious disposition it might safely be assumed that he would never have undertaken marriage had he not considered his position to be relatively secure. Two of his intimates have recounted what, in retrospect, seem amusing stories of his monetary difficulties in the eighties. One told how, on approaching Forain's studio, he saw piled up on the pavement a quantity of furniture and two easels. The artist was in debt and, unable to meet his obligations, was about to be sold up. The other said that on a further occasion Forain, knowing that his goods were about to be seized, hurriedly distributed all his household belongings among his friends and kept only a burning stove in his studio; this he invited the bailiff to take away.[36] Forain subsequently became one of the wealthiest artists in Paris and certainly one of the most hard-working. He earned his release from financial worries by the combination of his natural gifts with the strictest possible application. But again he showed an unexpected side to his character, for he was an inveterate gambler almost up to the last years. Perhaps such a painting as *Chambré*, reproduced in *le Figaro Illustré* of 1902, is an indication that playing at the tables was his favourite game of chance.

When Forain lived there, the rue Spontini was in one of the more modest *quartiers* of the city; since then, owing to its close proximity to the Bois, it has become one of the most fashionable streets in Paris. The house is now occupied by the famous couturier, M. Yves St Laurent, who takes pleasure in the knowledge that it continues to be used by an artist who still creates, though in a different medium.[37]

It seems very likely that Forain's marriage, with the changed domestic arrangements that followed in its wake, had something to do with his veering towards a new pictorial style. He had worked his way through one particular phase and now felt the promptings of a change within him; the need to tackle something fresh. An opportunity presented itself through his different and intimate mode of life in which he had his own 'models' around him, human beings with whom he was personally involved. Not since early youth had he known the warmth of family love and never before had there been anyone who looked to him for support. His position as a mere onlooker no longer pertinent, it was only natural that the unaccustomed emotions now awakened should steer him on to the course he was temporarily to take. For a time, and while romance and marriage were still excitingly novel experiences, Forain did a tender pastel of Jeanne as his fiancée (Plate ii) and then drawings and paintings of her as his wife and with their little son (Plates 38 and 39). But the family scene was not for him, and the pictures that form this group are few in number and not particularly assured, though of some importance in that they herald a more painterly style and form the link between the two phases of the painter's career.

The Mother and Child canvases, as also the Bedroom scenes, mark the end of the stylisation that was appropriate to the *Cocotte* series. For a short while the painter endeavoured to divorce himself from the satirist and became exclusively engrossed in those who comprised his daily life and whom he therefore knew in the most intimate way. When he discarded this theme in favour of the Law Courts which, to the end of his days, were to be by far the most important body of his work, a certain stylisation returned, but it was to be applied to wider and deeper social problems which affirmed Forain's concern for the great and little dramas that could shatter the lives of the poor and render them defenceless against the injustices of justice. Previously his had been an amused comment upon the lighter aspects of man's sensual appetites.

In the transitional Domestic canvases Forain attempted to wield the brush with as much freedom as he already handled chalk and as a result this small series of paintings is very sketchy. He was also becoming an almost complete monochromist. This is not to say that there are no middle-period paintings deprived of his favourite local colours, but they were becoming more and more rare. Moreover, he was drawing towards the low tones that were exclusively to characterise his Court-Rooms. Degas once wryly remarked that it was a pity that Sickert always painted 'at night', and here was his other close disciple and friend doing much the same. Leaving aside the question of overall quality, there are certain resemblances between Forain and Sickert. The outstanding characteristic that they shared was that of traditionalism. In the paintings of his maturity Forain, as already mentioned, went back to Holland of the seventeenth century and in particular to Frans Hals. Sickert's ancestry is extremely difficult to define. In his youth he was clearly Whistlerian, and that artist's fastidious sense of tonalities was implanted in him and remained with him throughout his life. After that there were echoes of Degas, for a short period a touch of Tintoretto, and even a flavour of the school of Munich. A curious medley which amounts to little in the understanding of the artist. Forain, despite his early attachment to Manet and his few *plein air* paintings, never sought to use light in the true Impressionist

33

terms; neither did Sickert, despite a small number of Pissarro-like canvases. Both were tonal painters but whereas Forain came virtually to eschew colour, Sickert chose a personal and subtle palette to which he always remained faithful. Forain was a rhetorical painter; Sickert would have it that he was too, but he used the subject as an excuse for picture-making while it was the actor in him, combined with his own ebullient humour, that led him to give, as an after-thought, fanciful titles to his works. Both men possessed what might be called a puritanical attitude towards their painting for in it neither indulged in revealing his emotion. Forain drew with angular strokes, parsimonical and decisive, while Sickert's drawings, not outstanding in themselves, were strongly suggestive of the canvases for which he would use them.

Although his paintings readily divide into two main groups, Forain occasionally plunged into unexpected waters and produced a few most surprising works. Such a one is the remarkably beautiful canvas *Mme Forain Pêchant à la Ligne* (Plate 37), also inspired by the family scene—painted with all the aplomb of the Impressionists in their own *plein air* field. Like many painters of his day, and as already stated, he had now and then been attracted towards *la Plage*, and the painting, *Une Promeneuse au Bord de la Mer* (Plate 20), as others in this small group, is close in conception to the series on the theme by Alfred Stevens. Like Manet, but more often Degas, Forain had occasionally been drawn towards *les Courses* (Plates 26–29), but it is *Mme Forain Pêchant à la Ligne* that is his masterpiece of the open air. Mme Forain is fishing—a form of relaxation that Forain frequently used as a subject for his drawings—while just behind her stands a nurse with the baby Jean-Loup in her arms, and further back a small dog rushes along the river's bank with ears flapping in the breeze. The figures placed in the centre of the canvas, though certainly the motivating interest, act pictorially as a point of focus and have no message to deliver. It was as if Forain had suddenly been impelled to let himself go in the joy of the event; as if all the years of censuring had been nonchalantly thrown aside, and all the years of studying crystallised. The palette in this painting is charming, the atmospheric effects delicately observed and realised. There is a wonderful feeling of stillness, of the peace of the country and its quiet, the only movement being the drifting of the clouds, the flight of the birds, and the bounding of the dog. Forain's whole life was devoted to the urban scene yet canvases such as this fill one with regret that he did not give himself to the practice of painting in all its facets.

Forain's lack of creativity as far as his own formal aims were concerned, together with his difficulty in developing to a final conclusion those suggested to him by the Masters, placed him in an awkward position as a painter. Around the turn of the century he was a man in his fifties, and he had lost his way. It has been said that when a cartoonist paints he does so as a kind of private activity, which, in essence, is true. But Forain regarded his painting as far more than a hobby and though for the moment he had reached an impasse, he searched for the solution to his problems with the admirable doggedness and persistence that since boyhood days had informed his varied activities. The situation was not easy: Forain was trying to be a 'Jack of two trades', one of which was most arduous and time-consuming. There is no hint—as there was with Daumier—of his ever having thought of relinquishing his journalistic *métier*. He had become a first-class draughtsman and in this sphere had carved a brilliant niche for himself. Besides, having known desperate poverty as a young bachelor, he was now earning a splendid living for his family and himself. Deeply attached to Degas, friends with artists in opposing camps and socially able to mix in two different worlds, Forain, the painter, was something of a schizophrenic. Was he to continue as an *Indépendant* or to become a Salon artist? He finally solved the problem by denying his allegiance to either.

The long drawn-out struggle that now ensued is evident in a large body of Forain's painting from this time onwards, specifically in his series on the Ballet, later the Atelier and finally the Gospel. It is only surprising that the artist, said to have been so critical of his own work and so ready to destroy, allowed these failures out into the world. Degas' most famous theme of Dancers was explored and turned to excellent account by his follower in his journalistic rôle; his attitude towards it was perfectly valid when it was used as a subject for social satire, for there was much to deplore in the situation of the little *rats de l'Opéra* forced by their parents to enter into this exigent world, generally for understandable though unworthy reasons. When Forain tried to turn these drawings into paintings it was usually a disaster for, instead of approaching the problem anew, he attempted to express one art-form in terms of another, for the more profound of which he had neither the ability as a painter nor the understanding of the student of ballet.

The pictures that were early in this series, mainly the little paintings and watercolours of *Danseuses dans leurs Loges* (Plates 24, 30, 31 and 33), retain a certain charm and humour, and were logically more successful because here Forain could introduce the slant that was his particular vision with a certain degree of authenticity. But even this acceptance contains some leniency for it supposes that Forain's 'incidents' took place after the fall of the curtain, when a performer is free to think of matters other than her work. He failed to realise, even in one of his better paintings of *Danseuses sur la Scène* such as *L'Entre Acte* (Plate VI), that once a dancer steps into the wings to await her entrance, she is wholly committed and has neither the time nor the inclination to dally with suitors. So, with the exception of a canvas like the earlier *Danseuses dans les Coulisses* (Plate 44), the pictures in this group are, in essence, untrue. Not only do they fail pictorially but they also offend, for they are a travesty of the beautiful and highly stylised art of ballet.

For about twenty years—roughly from 1885 until 1905—Forain persisted with these serio-comic girls in tutus surrounded by fat, lecherous and usually Semitic-looking men whose type was even more stressed after the Dreyfus Affair. Unlike Degas, Forain had no respect for the dancer, and in her world he was utterly out of his depth. It is well known how Degas attended the Opéra classes day after day, devoting himself to the minute study of the difficult technique of ballet until his understanding was profound and his failing eyes could no longer see. He has immortalised these *enfants de l'Opéra* because, one of the greatest draughtsmen of all time, he was also Master of the Dance and can never be surpassed. Forain exposed their situation through the columns of the press because it was for their predicament as human beings that he felt both compassion and scorn. There he should have left it.

Jeanne Forain and perhaps a few intimate friends were probably the only people aware of the dilemma that confronted Forain as he stood before his easel, and even they were seldom allowed to see what was going on. Forain always kept his studio door locked, even against his wife who had to resort to taking advantage of his absences when she was fortunate enough to find the hidden key. Once inside she found the atelier always the same: a myriad of canvases in different states of completion, piles of prints and drawings and all the tools of the artist's craft in the most astonishing disarray. She did not dare to touch a thing but, secretly locking the door again, left the dust of years and the heaps of rubbish to continue their accumulation.

Forain began his long association with *le Figaro* in 1893. It lasted, with one short break, for the remarkable period of thirty-one years, until a change in the paper's direction threatened the liberty he had always enjoyed and he resigned. In 1891 the *New York Herald* had devoted an entire supplement to his drawings, and as his work has long been admired in the States, American museums and private owners now possess by far the best collective group of his paintings, while a large number of drawings and prints are also in the country. In 1892 many of his drawings were published in Paris under the title *La Comédie Parisienne*; in the next year there appeared more volumes: *Album Forain, La Vie*, and *Nous, Vous, Eux*. Others followed, including *Le Doux Pays*, and besides *Psst . . . !* Forain also founded (1889–90) *Fifre* in order to 'Conter la vie de tous les jours, montrer le ridicule de certaines douleurs, la tristesse de bien des joies et constater rudement quelquefois par quelle hypocrite façon la vie tend à se manifester en nous . . .'.[38]

But in between all this work Forain was also able to enjoy himself, and when time permitted he indulged his love of travelling abroad. Vaillat says that Forain told him '. . . il [Forain] est allé à Londres pour assister au centenaire de la permission accordée aux catholiques de célébrer une messe en Angleterre',[39] and if this information is correct it means that Forain was in London on 24 June 1891, the centenary date of the Catholic Relief Act. Whether or not Forain made the occasion his excuse for a journey he already had in mind is impossible to say, but the reason given is somewhat suspect for there seem to be no other instances of such ardent orthodoxy on Forain's part. On one occasion, while on a visit to London—and it seems that he went more than once—Forain shaved off his beard. He was much teased about it by Degas for several years thereafter, and Sickert wrote that he remembered a clean-shaven Forain walking one night into the rue Victor Massé (Degas' home since 1890) immediately upon returning from a visit to England. 'We neither of us recognised the keen face which smacked at once of the bishop and the jockey, till we heard the agreeably grating tone of the well-known *traintane* voice: "Quoi, Monsieur Degas, en Angleterre l'homme bien est toujours rasé." "Eh bien, Monsieur Forain, en France c'est exactement le contraire. En France il n'y a que les domestiques qui sont rasés".'[40] Puget[41] reproduces a photograph of Forain called 'La cartomancienne', in which the artist is seated at a table, opposite him a fortune-teller, while standing behind him is Jeanne with her arms around his neck. As their wedding did not take place until 16 July 1891, and as Forain is still wearing his beard, this proves—endorsed by Colette's description of him around 1894—that he must have paid another visit to London after the latter date.

Forain went twice to the Middle East, stopping where fancy took him on the way—Italy, Greece, Palestine and the Lake Tiberius—and he is also said to have been to America. In 1914 he rushed to Leipzig to be with his friend

Hansi at his trial: '. . . qu'il ait au moins un Français au procès Hansi'.[42] It is notable, if Forain's words have been accurately quoted, that Hansi should have been a *Frenchman* and not simply a friend at a time of need. Nevertheless, Forain's gesture was a deeply considerate one. Even in his seventies he did not remain sedentary but travelled to Copenhagen, crossing Germany on a diplomatic passport. Two years later he was there again, this time to represent the Government at an exhibition and, on another official mission, he visited Naples as a member of the Institute. 1928 found him in Geneva, and even in the year before his death he went to Barcelona with his son. But more journeys have been mentioned—a 'return' to London at the unlikely early date of 1877 and a first visit to Italy in 1882, among others. The French as a nation are not notorious for their propensity to travel, believing, quite rightly, that theirs is one of the most beautiful countries in the world, and wrongly, that others have little to offer by comparison. Nobody could have been more nationalistic, even to the point of bigotry, than Forain, which gives credence to the Hansi remark, yet he had this desire to see other lands and would take off quite gaily and without any preparation should the opportunity present itself.

For a man who was politically a reactionary and artistically a traditionalist, Forain showed another unexpected taste—a penchant for all the latest modes of transport. '. . . j'ai toujours été passionné de nouveauté. J'ai voulu avoir la première bicyclette, le premier tandem, la première automobile'[43]—he also had one of the first telephones. There is that amusing incident in 1890 when he rode his tricycle along the road from Melun to welcome Degas and Bartholomé who were returning from a tour of Burgundy in a tilbury. What a droll picture this evokes: the frail white-bearded Degas tucked up in a rug, Bartholomé driving with one hand, the other in bandages as a result of poisoning, and a man of nearly forty riding to meet them on a tricycle! Only five years later the scene had completely changed, for Forain already possessed a motor-car which he christened 'Zedel' and with it, his own chauffeur. It was in this year of 1895 that the first real motor race took place; the course was from Paris to Bordeaux and back. Perhaps this was the event that fired Forain's imagination and prompted him to achieve his desire—an unusual one for an artist—of becoming a pioneer motorist. So enthusiastic did he continue that in 1901 he and Jeanne, the chauffeur driving, took part in one of the earliest international motor trials. Its route was from Paris to Berlin and of the 109 contestants who started, only 45 finished the course. Forain was not among them. He had had an accident on the way but all turned out well, even enjoyably, for nobody was hurt and they were rescued on the road by a Baron d'E., who invited them to his chateau in the vicinity, dined and wined them superbly, and persuaded them to stay the night.

Among the *petits maîtres* of the same genre as Forain whom he had met in his 'society' days in the salons of the '. . . femmes riches et de ces snobs entichés de peinture, de musique et de littérature . . .'[44] were Helleu, Boldini and Tissot. The latter was the eldest of the three and was already an established member of the beau-monde when Forain, who found it suited his purpose temporarily to play the dandy, was delighted to be accepted into such elevated circles. Later he was to repay his hosts and hostesses by castigating them in many drawings and paintings—see Notes to *l'Audition* (Plate V).

In his beginnings, Tissot had been influenced by Henry Leys, a second-rate Flemish painter of historical themes, and as a result he did some cheap but efficient 'costume' pictures. At the same time he produced an etched portrait of a young woman with all the realism of Courbet, and subsequently canvases in the manner of Whistler, Manet and Monet. In the middle sixties he painted a self-portrait which held great promise and which could even be, not too unfavourably, compared with Degas' famous Tissot portrait of about the same date. But Tissot did not fix his eyes upon quality; instead he became a Salon and Royal Academy exhibitor who won popularity as a Victorian painter, although he only lived in England for some ten years. The Goncourts scathingly referred to him as 'This ingenious exploiter of English idiocy . . .'.[45] From this it is clear that Tissot and Forain had nothing in common as artists, but they did meet when each painted a fashionable ballroom scene—the one in London, the other in Paris. Tissot's *Too Early* (Plate v)—the title itself says much—was exhibited at the Royal Academy in 1873, and although it has already been admitted that Forain's *Le Buffet* is completely academic, it is certainly the superior of the two. Both pictures are anecdotal in the extreme, but Forain has achieved a measure of characterisation in his *personnages* and interest in his composition, a certain quality in the handling of pigment as well as some degree of visual abstraction. In other words, he had a point of view. Tissot's painting is as tight, contrived and pretty as a fashion plate. Only the group in the left background suggests that its author had ever looked at a Degas, and even this corner is spoilt by the silly idea of the serving-girls peeping around the door. *Le Buffet* drops the hint that its creator might grow into a personality; *Too Early* states that half a dozen men of the period could have painted it.

Towards the end of their lives Tissot and Forain again found something in common when, curiously enough, each tried his hand at Religion as a theme for painting and etching. There is no need to dwell upon the results achieved by either: each series, in its own way, was disastrous, but whereas Tissot revealed a hollow lack of conviction, Forain's failure was due to his inability to realise a vision he longed to, or perhaps did, feel deeply. At least his mistakes were those of an artist.

Paris being the Mecca for painters from Europe and the USA, the young Paul Helleu included among his friends several who had come there, directly or indirectly, from their native countries—Whistler and Sargent, the Americans, Stevens the Belgian, and Boldini the Italian. Sargent, ever generous, took Helleu under his wing and '. . . like an elder brother he helped build Helleu's career'[46] with an attachment that remained undiminished throughout the years. But the mysterious light and masculine solidity of London also created artist Anglophiles, and after a visit to London Helleu agreed with two others of his friends, Tissot and Jacques-Emile Blanche, that 'L'Angleterre est magnifique, splendide, grandiose . . .'.[47] Helleu shared Boldini's adoration for elegance and beauty in women: 'La laideur lui inspirait une sorte d'horreur epouvantée, emerveillée aussi.'[48] This passion was to be the key to Helleu's worldly success and, it must be admitted, to his artistic tenuity. Of him Degas is reported to have said— although it is denied by some biographers—'C'est du Watteau à vapeur',[49] and, no doubt influenced by the Goncourts, Helleu did develop a taste for the eighteenth century and, in particular, for that exquisite painter. To Watteau's studies of women's heads he paid homage in the innumerable drawings with which his name is irrevocably linked; he also used Watteau's characteristic and attractive medium known to the *cognoscenti* as *trois crayons*. These drawings, as well as his etchings of beautiful women, brought him enormous success both in commissions and in sales, but Helleu's paintings were not liked. He had a predilection for whites, clear blues and yellows at a time when lower-toned pictures were preferred—a preference that the Impressionists also knew to their cost. Marcel Proust, who disliked Forain but loved Helleu, used the latter as his prototype for the artist in *A la Recherche du Temps Perdu*. Proust made Elstir a fashionable portraitist who painted in blue and yellow and who was also, as Helleu became, a painter of harbour scenes and yachts. To this day Helleu's canvases are even less known than Forain's; each attained his own notoriety through a very different approach to draughtsmanship. Any appreciable collection of Helleu's facile drawings and prints brings forth a sigh of utter boredom; singly they have a certain charm, while those of his wife and children are diffused with a real tenderness. Despite his artistic failings Helleu evokes sympathy, for he so evidently enjoyed drawing *les femmes à la mode de la Belle Epoque* who earned him so handsome a living. There seems little doubt that he knew these drawings for what they were but could not resist doing them. This is a pity, because his light-filled *Yachts* and *Bassins*, handled with freedom, with flowing pigment and long tenuous brush-strokes, suggest the possibility of better things. As an artist he had no affinity with Forain; they were poles apart, and so it is amusing to find even one picture by each where slight similarities may be detected. Helleu's *Femme Etendue sur une Banquette* (Plate vii) has a certain awkwardness which gives it an unusual and welcome character. The silhouetted figure of the reclining woman against the back of the bench echoes the shape of the couch in Forain's smaller and earlier canvas of a similar subject, *Femme à l'Eventail sur un Canapé* (Plate 8). In both, the picture planes are divided horizontally into three areas connected by an oblique arrangement of stresses from the upper left to the lower right, and both give nice suggestions of ambiance. Forain's model is a pert, perhaps slightly wicked, young woman; Helleu's is an amused young lady enjoying relaxation. Here ends the resemblance between the piquant painter of the *cocotte* and the gentle portraitist of the beau-monde.

Although born in Ferrara, Boldini—the 'Casanova of Painting'—exemplified, in all their extravagance, the mood and fashions of the Belle Epoque. He had studied in Florence, had enjoyed immediate success during a stay in London, and from 1872, having decided to settle in Paris, he soon became the rage of its smart society. His tiny study in oil paint of *Diego Martelli* (Plate ix) of 1867 shows an unexpected reticence, for Boldini was already becoming enamoured of the effect of brilliant vitality that flashing sweeps of a loaded brush could suggest in the most quiescent sitter. Degas painted his own famous portrait of the stouter *Martelli* (Plate xi) just twelve years after Boldini had done his. For a while the two artists had been intimate —another incongruous friendship; each made a drawing of the other, and in 1889 they travelled together in Spain and Tangier. Boldini's drawing of *Degas* (Plate x), in oil upon canvas, was evidently the project for a painting that never materialised; perhaps a good thing, for the drawing is finely controlled, the figure beautifully placed—obviously under the influence of the sitter—and for Boldini, it is almost unique in its weight and scale. As both he and Helleu were ardent admirers of feminine beauty each, because more detached, produced better works of art when painting male sitters: their individual portraits of Whistler are but one example. As Boldini adored women so he, as an artist, was lionized by them. They were responsible for his triumphant success and this is by no means surprising, for he transformed the most ordinary into *femmes fatales* giving them a sparkle and glamour that they rarely, if ever, possessed. A sure recipe for a portrait painter. Apart from finding themselves temporarily in the same milieu, Boldini by choice and Forain mainly by necessity, there was no aesthetic rapport between these two and therefore no need to comment upon the difference between the two portraits of young women each artist painted, within two or three years of the other, in the early eighties (Plates xii and 5). Degas summed up Boldini probably more succinctly than anyone else: 'Mon cher Boldini, quel grand talent vous avez, mais quelle drôle idée vous avez de l'humanité: quand vous faites un homme, vous le ridiculisez; et quand vous faites une femme, vous la déshonorez!'[50]

The most delightful painter among Forain's acquaintances was another Italian-born artist, Giuseppe de Nittis. He died at the early age of thirty-eight, so that his output was necessarily small and his work, therefore, much prized. The guest standing, holding a cup and saucer, on the right of *Le Buffet* is said to have been de Nittis; if this is so he must have posed to Forain a matter of months before his death. In Florence, de Nittis became one of the group known as *I Macchiaioli* who, in the manner of the Paris artists, met at their chosen café and comprised the most 'advanced' painters of the day. After the Franco-Prussian war he settled in Paris but repeatedly returned to the Italian countryside that he loved. He is known for his charming street scenes of Italian cities as well as those of London and Paris. Sensitive, delicate paintings peopled with tiny, fastidiously placed figures, they are as calm and untroubled as his scenes of refugees fleeing from the erupting Mount Vesuvius are, within his *oeuvre*, dramatic. De Nittis loved life and this *joie de vivre*, one of his most appealing traits, shone through his work and was in direct contrast with Forain's attitude to the world. But Forain too had his gentle moments, and in one of them he painted the little domestic scene, *Après Diner* (Plate viii), of the middle eighties which he inscribed to a patron or friend. De Nittis' happy *Jeune Femme Assise au Bord du Lac* (Plate vi) has the same underlying firmness of drawing and mastery of handling as this watercolour of Forain's; both are suffused with a gentle feeling of repose and while the mood is nostalgic, it has not been allowed to become oversweet. In each picture the concentration is focused upon the figure of the young woman, who does not stand out in isolation but is harmoniously related to her surroundings.

Among both the genre painters and the *humoristes*, Théophile Steinlen emerges, not as one of the most gifted artists, but as one of the most interesting personalities. Increasing literacy had started a vogue for illustrated books and journals. Industrial developers were beginning to realise the importance of advertising manufactured goods, and theatrical impresarios the value of publicity—hence the coloured poster was born, and Cheret was its father. Unlike his colleagues, Steinlen had received no academic training. Born in Lausanne in 1859, he became an apprentice in a textile factory where he worked in the designing section. In 1881 he managed to get to Paris where Willette introduced him to Rodolphe Salis, the proprietor of Le Chat Noir, a cabaret where writers and painters were wont to gather. Here, among others, Steinlen met Lautrec, Forain and Caran d'Ache. He made drawings of cats for the cabaret's journal and their fame became such that Steinlen was forthwith labelled *le peintre des chats*, much to the detriment of his reputation as a serious artist. Gradually other commissions came: illustrations for novels, satirical drawings for newspapers, as well as posters of all kinds—a beginning parallel to that of Forain. Steinlen, too, was imbued with a deep sense of social justice, not quickened as was the French conscience by successive political upheavals but born, no doubt, of his close proximity to the workers in the Mulhouse factory. Unlike Forain he was not a splendid draughtsman, neither was it his intention to 'witness and expose'. His observations were kinder and more generous and if his drawings were not as decisive, neither was their timbre as acid nor their view so bigoted. Steinlen is not an easy artist to define; his *écriture* is somewhat anonymous, and spattered through his work are gleams of Daumier, Millet and other contemporaries including the Norwegian, Munch. By nature he was a humanist and the works by which he will finally be remembered are those such as the touching *les Pauvres Gens* (Plate xiii), who are wondering whether prison might not be warmer than their bitterly cold street bench, and *le 14 Juillet* (Plate xiv) in which, for a brief annual moment, the working-class couples, forgetting their petty squabbles and real deprivations, link arms in comradeship and, like puppets obeying the intoxicating spirit of the fête, sing and dance under the *lampions*. In 1911 Steinlen, together with Forain and Willette, founded the journal *les Humoristes* and about the same date Steinlen drew the well-observed portrait of Forain (Plate xix) which makes

43

a telling comparison with the latter's *Self-portrait* (Plate xxi). Forain, looking in the mirror, has seen a scowling, pessimistic face; Steinlen, a more charitable soul, has been impressed by the keen look, the glint in the eye and the play of humour around the mouth. The assured thriftiness of line enhanced by swift washes of the brush show absolute mastery in the *Self-Portrait,* whereas Steinlen's more positive outlook has only been realised with a certain amount of searching. 'La qualité de l'art de Steinlen n'était pas malheureusement à l'échelle de ses sentiments. . . .'[51]

There are only a few isolated exceptions to the rule that all painters start by following in somebody else's footsteps: Degas began with Ingres, Monet with Boudin, Gauguin with the Impressionists, and Van Gogh with Millet. Today these 'followers' are Old Masters and so it is known how wonderfully each developed his personal aesthetic and formulated an entirely new way of expressing it. Nobody would dream of comparing Forain with any of these great figures. Admittedly his main energies were channelled into another field, but if the urge to paint had been deadly urgent, nothing in the world could have stopped his giving every moment to its practice. It is therefore profitless to speculate upon what he might have become had this happened. All the same, and unpredictable though he undoubtedly was, Forain's volte-face as a painter seems, at first impact, to defy explanation—it is a kind of Van Gogh story in reverse. In middle life he not only repudiated the authority that Manet and Degas had exercised over him but also chose to ignore all the daring experiments and amazingly varied achievements with which the contemporary art world was then seething. The revolt against Impressionism, first signalled about 1884, had truly opened the flood-gates of creativeness, and the fecundity of the following two decades was of such astonishing richness as to give an excuse for recalling, once again, some of its most outstanding events.

By the mid nineties Cézanne, the 'father of modern painting', the man who had bowed to architecture as the mistress of the visual arts, was established in Provence; Degas was working on his last great series, the austere and sculpturesque Nudes, and Monet had still to paint his *Nymphéas*. Gauguin, having gone native in Tahiti, had left Paris for ever; Van Gogh's brilliant, but incredibly short, span had ended in tragedy some five years before; Lautrec, with only a few more years ahead, was painting and drawing his favourite characters of the theatre, music-hall and circus. Seurat, having perfected his important discovery of Divisionism, had died shortly after Van Gogh, at the age of thirty-two, and the Douanier Rousseau, the Primitive of wonderful imagination and fantasy, was reaching towards his zenith. The mind is overwhelmed by such a galaxy of talents. And there were startling names to follow, for Matisse and Rouault were in Gustave Moreau's studio, Bonnard was exhibiting with the *Nabis*, and in Spain Picasso, at the age of fourteen, had painted a remarkably precocious canvas.

Forain had all this going on around him, all this creativity from which to gain inspiration. Up till now he had talked with an accent of his own but what he had had to say had already been voiced by others. Having reached the half-way point in his painting life he had worked through his apprenticeship to his two great masters, and being a man of lively intelligence with a concern for the more serious aspects of life, the superficialities of the Belle Epoque no longer appealed to him. But what was he going to do? His art had not developed naturally and of its own volition into any independent personal expression for, sadly enough, his powers of imagination in front of the easel had not grown with the years. As a satirical draughtsman situations were presented to him and they evoked a response; no such parallel is enjoyed by the painter—his inspiration has to come from within, and in Forain's case it was not there to draw upon. Once again he would have to turn to another's inventiveness and imbue it with his own characteristics. This decision was probably not quite as deliberate as it may sound, for history has a way of compressing and simplifying facts.

In terms of the history of art, the choice made by Forain is so at variance with other known examples that it inevitably comes as a shock. It would, indeed, be extremely difficult to quote an instance of a more reactionary step than the one he decided to take. There is little evidence—always excepting Degas—to show what Forain thought of the individual important painters working during his lifetime, but it is known that he disliked Monet, both the man and the artist, and that, among sculptors, he found Rodin inferior to Rude. But remembering that he was by nature and profession an artist dedicated to the 'black and white', that he thought '. . . sont splendides tous les tons de la grisaille', then it is understandable that he did not 'hitch his wagon' to any of the stars who comprised the living French scene. He was a man who had come to distrust colour, and this at a time when colour was becoming a more and more important factor in the story of picture-making. Scientifically, Seurat had explored it to its climax; aesthetically, Matisse was to discover its pure and decorative possibilities and his findings were to channel

45

art into the non-representational idiom of the post Second World War period. But beyond all, Forain was a story-teller, and the subject picture had begun its steady decline and was to disappear altogether from the *avant-garde* scene until the advent of 'Pop-Art' re-introduced it some seventy years later.

After the birth and development of Impressionism, contemporary thought became more and more focused upon formal aesthetics: Divisionism, Nabi-ism, Fauvism, Negroism, Cubism, Futurism, and so on until the present day. Forain was not a theoretical man nor one to fit in with such rapidly changing events. He was no daring innovator but a conservative who preferred the well-trod path.

The total recognition that had evaded Daumier during his lifetime was slowly granted after his death in 1879. Exhibitions, official purchases, articles in the press and public auctions all added to this posthumous triumph. They culminated in 1893 with the sale of the Geoffrey-Dechaume Collection which comprised no less than 3,500 lithographs, some drawings, and above all, paintings of every period. Daumier was finally acknowledged, not only as a satirist-draughtsman but also as a painter of considerable stature. '. . . Daumier redevient le Maître des caricaturistes. Forain, Willette, d'autres encore le considèrent comme leur dieu',[52] and in 1894 Forain published in the *Courrier Français* 'La Femme Somnambule' in imitation of, and as an act of homage to, the artist who had died fifteen years before. In view of his own uncertain situation at the time, of his natural compulsion towards reform, together with the fact that he, too, was trying to practise the same two disparate branches of art, it was almost inevitable that Forain should have chosen Daumier as his guide and prop. Moreover, his assessment had been confirmed by Degas who not only cherished the beautiful Daumier painting and hundreds of lithographs he had in his collection but had also, through some of his own work, given positive proof of his admiration.

Daumier began his career by doing lithography and he became probably the greatest, and certainly the most prolific, lithographer of all time. Born in Marseilles in 1808 he, like Victor Hugo, was to live through no less than three revolutions. Taken to Paris while still a boy, just after the fall of Napoleon, he was in the capital during the Revolution of the Three Days, the particularly bloody disasters of 1848, and finally during the Siege and the Commune. Having been placed as an errand boy to a bailiff at the age of thirteen, his familiarity with the visual aspects of the legal world not surprisingly led and gave conviction to the series of *Avocats* with which his name is as readily associated as Degas' with ballet and Lautrec's with brothels.

Daumier's passion for the drama may well have begun in childhood with the production of his father's one and only play, but it was while he worked as a clerk in a bookshop near the Comédie-Français, in the Palais-Royal, that he not only developed it seriously—together with a liking for actors—but became even more intrigued by the extraordinary medley of faces among the crowds that gathered in the famous galleries of Balzac's 'bazaar ignoble'.[53] The imaginative, quiet young man whose only ambition was to draw, was enthralled by his daily experience of watching this herd, so that his natural leaning towards the comic flourished and developed into a positive infatuation for the grimace. These characters, as well as the lawyers, were later to comprise his main scene.

Towards the end of the 1820s there was an enormous demand for caricature prints and in 1829 the first satirical weekly in France, *La Silhouette*, made its début. Daumier became a revolutionary caricaturist and his drawings were soon a sensation. So formidable were they that he was arrested in 1832 for the attack on Louis-Phillipe that he had published in *La Caricature*, of which paper Balzac was the editor. The great writer was quick to recognise the artist's talent and worth as a man and they became lifelong friends. Daumier had also started modelling. In this endeavour he met with more success than did the youthful Forain, but although his small figures are topically expressive, sculpturally they are much over-esteemed. The first to dare to ridicule political personages in this medium—again the subject was Louis-Phillipe, as well as Thiers and others—Daumier's later and most famous figurine of the Bonapartist agent, Ratapoil, had to be hidden as a subversive work.

In prison, the fearless Daumier began to paint upon the walls of his cell the same pictorial attacks that had led to his arrest. The under-privileged, *les Filibustiers parisiens*, were the players in his particular *Comédie Humaine*, so that besides the approval of Balzac, Daumier also won the admiration of Baudelaire. The poet and the painter also became devoted to each other, for Daumier possessed a great gift for friendship and his wide circle included some of the most famous writers, painters, musicians and actors of that memorable period. Once free from prison Daumier lived in a community of artists and for several years was influenced by the now-forgotten Jeanron and the then-popular Decamps. Remote from all traces of Classicism he, like his friend Delacroix, came under the Rubens influence and he even made a copy of the latter's *Kermesse*. While Rubens' robust figures informed Daumier's paintings only until about the middle fifties, he never relinquished the Flemish master's feeling for action, to which he normally added a greater exaggeration of gesture. But like all individualists it was not long before his own personality began to emerge and his work became easily recognisable. Daumier preferred large-scale figures which he imbued with a sometimes mocking nobility, and he lit them with theatrical effect to illuminate their contorted features and to silhouette the vigour of their forms. This use of chiaroscuro made an important contribution towards the tremendous intensity of the whole. He had the tendency to leave his paintings in a sketchy state, perhaps out of preference or else because he was unable to carry them further. Forain, too, left many sketchy pictures—many unsolved—but this was certainly not out of choice, as his best late canvases bear witness to the fine and complete conclusion he was able to sustain when at the height of his powers. It is more than likely that both artists meant to return to their *inachevées* paintings but that there was seldom time, for both were haunted by the inexorable date of going to press and Daumier's livelihood, as Forain's after him, depended upon journals. Daumier was thought by fellow artists to be in the first rank of painting and he longed to give his full time to it. As far as is known, Forain—despite his regard for the high worth of oil painting—never even considered this possibility.

Daumier's impact upon many important artists who followed is perhaps greater than is generally realised; from among them the one who concerns this story is Degas, the link between Daumier and Forain. Daumier it was who discovered the theatre with all its magical unreality, charged expectancy, drama, escapism—its total atmosphere. The world of difference between his Romanticism and the cool restrained Classicism of Degas needs no comment, but the relationship in several instances between the specific theme and compositional arrangements of these two men, which might be supposed to have originated with Degas, are far too marked to have been fortuitous. Daumier's famous *Le Mélodrame* (Plate xvi) of about 1860 pre-dates Degas' first version of *l'Orchèstre de l'Opéra* (Plate xv)—the beginning of his 'audience and stage' paintings—by about ten years; and whether one accepts Mr Maison's or M. Adhémar's later dating *les Lutteurs* precedes Degas' earliest canvases of a complete stage scene by very much longer. The unusual conception of Daumier's *l'Homme à la Corde* (Plate xviii), also of about 1860, must surely have prompted Degas' *Mlle Lala au Cirque Fernando* (Plate xvii) of around nineteen years later, as must have the few *Blanchisseuses*, so beauti-fully echoed and developed by Degas several years after Daumier's death. The rapport between these two great men is just one of the fascinating aspects in the contemplation of the history of art for, separated by the gap of a generation, each was fervent about movement, the one emotionally, the other scientifically.

Daumier worked for *Charivari* for more than twenty years as Forain worked, even longer, for *le Figaro*, and the public waited expectantly for his drawings as later they were to do for those of the younger man. Although one was a revolutionary and the other a reactionary, each had a moral con-science which led him to champion the under-privileged by castigating their oppressors. But being of an expansive nature and of genial disposition, in fact a man much loved, Daumier, although violent against injustice, en-couraged his readers to laugh as well as to think. Baudelaire wrote: 'J'ai voulu dire que le génie satirique de Daumier n'avait rien de commun avec le génie satanique . . .'.[54]

In his later years Daumier grew ever closer in friendship to the Barbizon painters, and above all to Millet. Following these kindly, nature-loving artists came Renoir, Pissarro and Monet, but side by side with these were also the essentially urban figures of Degas, Lautrec and Forain. Of these last three each was a man of culture, each possessed an intellect that could be distinctly acid, and as Daumier was affectionately known as *le buveur du bon boc* so Forain might be called *le buveur du vinaigre*.

Daumier's Court paintings were surprisingly few in number—less than twenty—and but for one scene inside the Palais de Justice, they comprise studies of advocates. They were much spread out in date, ranging from the middle forties until about 1870. But his drawings and especially his litho-graphs on the theme were numerous, more ambitious in their inventiveness and therefore more elaborate in composition. *Le Grand Escalier du Palais de Justice* has, for instance, an almost Raphael-like nobility of conception although it is, in fact, a very small painting. Pictorially, Daumier felt his message to be so evident that, unlike Forain, he regarded *légendes* as superfluous and seldom wrote his own. As a draughtsman, his most recognisable tendency was to employ a 'doodling' action with his pen or pencil, like a sculptor feeling his way over the surface of a rippling form. The whole was then brought together and clarified by emphatic, incisive strokes which define the more pertinent characteristics of the figures. This particular technique may sound accidental, but in Daumier's hands it was a deliberate manner of working.

By 1902 Forain was painting the Court-Room scenes with which his name has now become as closely associated as Daumier's. The series reached its zenith between about 1907 and 1911; after that there were intermittent oils, drawings in chalk, and lithographs, the last being a painting as late as 1930. This final *Procès* clearly reveals the failing powers of an old and sick man, but beyond that it is a touching example of the gallantry of an artist determined to work until the very end. He died in the following year.

Soon after the turn of the century Forain confined himself to warm mono-chromatic tones—relieved occasionally by one splash of colour—whose transitions he handled with particular beauty. In the best of these canvases, dark browns and blacks give both depth and richness and, in the manner of Daumier, they are also used to stress Forain's typical, angular drawing, so different from the roundness of the master. The highlights, applied last of all, emblazon features according to the degree of their owner's importance in the composition; they define a prominent cheek-bone, a hooked nose or a towering forehead. With the certainty of drawing as its foundation, the brush is wielded with a Hals-like bravura; with a sketchy but penetrating accuracy it characterises all the players in the drama, through the tension of their bodies as much as through their wonderfully expressive hand gestures and anxious, sometimes despairing faces. With but very rare exceptions Forain painted the trial in progress, that is to say that his advocates are seen within the setting of the Palais de Justice. He also had a great liking for crowds. His compositions nearly all follow the habitual pattern: prominent figures in the lower half of the picture-plane cut horizontally by the edge of the canvas or by a table, the whole divided somewhere across the middle, usually by the partition behind which the defendant and onlookers are seated. This was an arrangement directly attributable to Daumier as may be seen by comparing his watercolour drawing *Le Défenseur* (Plate xx) with Forain's far more ambitious oil *Scène de Tribunal* (Plate 45). The difference between the media is of little importance in these two typical works which succinctly contrast the histrionic approach of the one artist with the near-realism of the other. Both men considered the lawyer to be '... un homme qui abuse de la crédulité du public'.[55] Daumier's *Avocat* is indicating to his client: 'I have done my best, your case is lost—je m'en fiche!' All gestures and expressions are larger than life. But Forain, to some extent and because of a more natural-istic intention, involves one in the tragic plight of his defendant who, in desperation, puts in one final plea as his lawyer is about to leave the court. *Scène de Tribunal* is one of those compositions in which all is on the horizontal, relieved but by the suggestion of a column, a vertical panel or by one upstanding figure. Sometimes a commanding 'upright' person rises from the darkness to draw the design up into a triangle, such as *le Prétoire* (Plate 48) and *La Fille-Mère* (Plate 50), or to form a bold, diagonal line as in *Audience de Tribunal* (Plate VII) and *l'Avocat Général* (Plate VIII). There is a considerable feeling of release and certainty in these last four canvases in comparison with the earlier and more tentative ones. Daumier was fond of linking his lawyer with other figures in the trial by a great flourishing gesture of his arm. The pointed finger could be accusing; the upturned hand, pleading. Forain has used a similar device in *Condamner à Perpétuité* (in the Art Institute of Chicago). The prisoner is poignantly kissing the hand of his counsel, presumably because he has escaped the death penalty, while the lawyer, with a Daumier-like grimace, mockingly accepts the tribute. These splendid paintings of Forain's are more restrained than Daumier's and less immediate. The latter possessed that degree of clumsiness, the trait of many a great artist; he courageously distorted in order to achieve his full impact, and carried abstraction to a high degree. Forain was inclined to be more polished and specific and lacked that extra spark that was the master's. Daumier drew in paint; Forain, in this series, was entirely a painter and, in contrast with his beginnings, the larger the scale the more successful are his Court-Rooms. At their best they can hold their own in the company of all but the great.

'Among those who knew him slightly . . . [he] was reputed to be irascible, ill-mannered, and virtually inaccessible. His friends and colleagues, on the other hand, always described him as considerate, warm-hearted and extremely hospitable . . . strangers or casual acquaintances who tried to intrude on his privacy were assured of a chilly reception.'[56] These words might well have been written about Degas; instead, they were describing Huysmans and are not absolutely impertinent in relation to Forain himself. As the story of Huysmans' life has become well-known through much research and many extant letters, it is strange that so little documentary evidence exists regarding his association with the painters who were in his circle in the early years, and a particular pity that there is nothing to explain the long break in his friendship with Forain.

In the winter of 1900 Huysmans, who was then an oblate at Ligugé and already suffering from the painful bouts of neuralgia that were to plague him until the end of his days, received a telegram from Forain announcing that the artist would join him on Christmas Eve. There is no doubt that Huysmans was delighted, for he wrote: 'Christmas Eve was magnificent here, and made more memorable for me by a truly joyous event. Just imagine—I'd seen nothing of the painter Forain for twenty years, although I'd heard vague rumours that he'd returned to the Church, when suddenly, on Christmas Eve, I had a telegram from him asking if I could put him up for the night; I wired him to come, and later saw the wicked old rascal of old taking Communion at Midnight Mass. It was certainly an odd experience for two friends who had been sceptics together and gone on the spree together in Paris, to meet again after so many years . . . at midnight, in the church at Ligugé.'[57] What a nice ending to their story, for Forain's startling telegram and the immediacy of Huysmans' reply prove that the friendship was so real that, despite a quarrel or merely a drifting apart, it could be joyfully resumed with apparently no questions asked and no recriminations made after so long a period. From then on the two remained close to each other and when, six years later, Huysmans was dying of cancer and in the greatest pain, he 'found comfort . . . in the visits of his dearest friends',[58] of whom Forain was one.

Following the custom of their day, both Huysmans and Forain had been brought up as Catholics. That each should have become a sceptic was not abnormal, for young people generally go through a phase of questioning and, in any case, their minds are set on material matters when enjoyment of life and plans for the future occupy them to the exclusion of nearly everything else. Forain, moreover, was possibly reacting against the pious M. Jacquesson de la Chevreuse.

Of the two, Huysmans was a man of far greater complexity: he had gone through brief periods of homosexual tendencies, suffered phases of impotence and had a horror of marriage, all perhaps due to an early difficult relationship with his mother. He had delved into the experiences of life both worthy and unworthy, sordid, decadent and dangerous. Aesthetic to a degree, even in his approach to the Church—he adored sacred music—he became much concerned with the state of his soul and desperately desired to 'believe': 'Still too much the man of letters to make a monk, yet already too much the monk to remain among men of letters.'[59] In 1892 he felt that at last he could 'knock at God's door' but not until six years later did he make preparations to retire from the world he had known. He did not, however, commit himself entirely but chose to live as a secular priest. Huysmans finally came to peace through 'attainment' and met his death with saintly acceptance.

Forain seems to have undergone much less of a spiritual struggle: '. . . ma piété est venue d'avoir vécu au pied de la Cathédrale. J'avais cinq ou six ans . . . Vers l'âge de dix-huit ans, la vie parle . . . Cette folie dura jusque vers trente-cinq ans; alors, la foi vint en moi d'un seul coup et elle n'a plus fait que grandir.'[60] Taken at its face value this statement sounds like a gross over-simplification, for this greatest of human experiences does not flash as a stroke of lightning illuminating life for the rest of time; its growth is slow and often unsuspected '. . . the sudden emergence into consciousness of a very gradual process'.[61] Despite, perhaps because of, his worldly success, Forain must have been suffering some inner dissatisfaction which refused to be dispelled by any material solution and just as Huysmans' struggles had led him towards the Light, so Forain hoped to find artistic salvation through his newly found Faith.

He returned from Ligugé 'réconforté et rassemblé pour des traveux d'art plus dignes . . . tout ce que j'ai fait jusqu'à présent en art me semble choses vaines et je sens que je n'aurai de repos que quand j'aurai confessé et manifesté ma Foi avec les moyens que Dieu m'a donne [sic] . . .',[62] and he begged Huysmans to pray that he might become 'un artiste chrétien'. Three more unpublished letters passed between the friends at this time; Forain complained that his journalistic work, and above all 'la sale vie de Paris' prevented any peaceful contemplation; he said that he wanted to paint the departure of the Virgin after Christ had been placed in the tomb and everything was over. He could imagine the effect, the atmosphere and even the tonality, but neither the style of the figures nor their expressions. He felt himself lacking the necessary power and conviction; he also feared that this lack was born of his bad habits in the past and his cowardice in the present. Huysmans replied with understanding and sympathy; he had been through the same experiences himself. Forain must have patience, he must pray: 'Vous pouvez bien penser une chose, c'est que si Dieu vous a ramené à Lui, comme il a fait pour moi, c'est pour que nous lui soyons, selons la mesure de nos pauvres forces, utiles; il vous en donnera donc ainsi qu'à moi les moyens.'[63] But '. . . God fulfils himself in many ways . . .' and to some extent Forain did achieve his desire, albeit not in the manner he had envisaged. Unlike Huysmans he was never destined to discard his worldly interests. He had a wife and child to keep—Jean-Loup was only six years old—and he was too deeply involved to throw aside his journalistic commitments. The longing to break with the past appears sincerely felt, but compared with Huysmans' spiritual anguish, it was on a different level. But there was to be a change. Forain's satires for the press were, from then until the 1914–18 war, confined to social problems, and his paintings took on a new dimension. His growing realisation of Daumier had coincided with his spiritual seeking, so warmly encouraged and understood by Huysmans, and he fused the influences of these two men and attained his highest achievements as a painter. Through his Court-Rooms he became 'un artiste chrétien', for he was able to instil into them a kindlier compassion than had hitherto informed his work— compassion for the poorer folk at the mercy of the law. Compared with the charming frivolities of the early years, they may truly be said to be 'des traveaux d'art plus dignes' although it is doubtful as to whether Forain ever regarded them as such.

Whatever struggles may have tormented him in the studio, Fate was clearly indicating that Forain was not to retire into the quietness of seclusion, for now professional successes were gaining momentum. He had already been made a Chevalier de la Légion d'honneur and in the year after his return from Ligugé, *le Figaro Illustré* devoted an entire number to his work in which two of the earliest Court-Room scenes and the first of his Religious pictures were reproduced together with a selection of other paintings and drawings. The variety of subjects shows how wide was Forain's range—café concerts of the eighties, *les Courses*, *les Coulisses de l'Opéra*, satires in oil on the *Soirée Musicale* and *l'Expert de Tableaux*, portrait drawings, social comments and a casino interior. In 1904 he entered into an agreement with the Paris gallery of Bernheim-Jeune to let them have fifty canvases within the space of one year and at the rate of four a month. An impossible undertaking unless, as is more than likely, Forain had sold few paintings to date and was therefore able to supply the majority from his atelier. In 1909 the same gallery staged a Forain exhibition—the first comprehensive one ever to have been held, for it comprised not only drawings and prints but also oils. Forain had been accepted as a painter. There is no doubt that he enjoyed the sweetness of worldly acclaim with its accompanying material wealth.

But now he realised that he must and could get away from Paris for at least part of each year, so he bought a delightful Directoire house at le Chesnay, its spacious grounds filled with beautiful tall trees and bordering upon the park of Versailles. This property was a joy to him; there, he and his family spent the best part of the summer months away from all the bustle and noise of the city, and there he installed his printing press.

Despite the splendour of his lithographs they had met with scant success and in 1908, disappointed by their failure to please, Forain returned to etching after having abandoned that medium for some eighteen years. The majority of these etchings were devoted to the much acclaimed Religious series, but there were also some Court-Rooms and portraits. He engraved a posthumous portrait of Huysmans two years after his friend's death in 1907, either from memory or from a lost drawing (Plate xxiv). He did a tentative one of himself seated beside Jean-Loup at the piano, and as he was leading a very private life during his summers in the country, it is not surprising that he became his own chief model. He etched at least five self-portraits, not all successful plates yet all revealing that the eye was just as penetrating as it had been in the earlier lithograph portraits: *Forain Lithographe* (Plate iv), three in different positions of the infirm Renoir of 1905 (Plate xxiii), and that of the celebrated art dealer Ambroise Vollard made about 1910. Bonnard painted one of the famous dinners held in Vollard's *Cave*; in this, among other guests, Cézanne, Renoir, Redon and Forain are included.

Forain continued to paint Dancers, occasional Nudes and a series of Artist and Model compositions—the latter, sad canvases of a despairing artist, pictorially weak and too obviously contrived. Yet he persisted in these with a sheer tenacity that amounted almost to fanaticism. He was determined to solve this particular self-imposed challenge, which he never did, but what was the underlying motive? He is known to have thought that only a painting in oils was worthy of consideration as a serious work of art; drawings and *aquarelles* were lightweight, perhaps because both media, through natural talent and unceasing practice, came brilliantly and easily to him—though he never became a virtuoso. Did this particular Studio theme constitute a symbol of his own struggles with a far more demanding medium, and in addition, did it represent the problems that inevitably face the artist who, having habitually painted from drawings, is suddenly confronted with the model before him?

The Evangelical idea, born at Ligugé, lived on in Forain's mind until the end of his days. In December 1930, only seven months before his death, Daniel Halévy wrote that he saw him 'Tragic in his extreme old age—coughing, spitting . . .' but still trying to finish a *Christ Standing Trial*.[64]

Back in Paris after having left Huysmans, Forain immediately and eagerly started trying to translate the great Christian saga of the past into an idiom of his own. But helpless without a prototype he turned to the Old Masters—in etching, particularly to Rembrandt—for understandably, Daumier's early religious paintings, even the huge and splendid *Barabbas*, were too experimental and too few in number to be of use to him. So Forain never resolved the Old and New Testaments in terms of oil paint and no one realised it better than he, but still he went on trying. Actually, the situation was back to front, for the subject was firmly established though the formal aim was unknown.

Forain's prints from the Gospel were applauded and they brought him fresh triumphs as an engraver. From some writers they brought the extravagant praise that in this medium he was the equal of Rembrandt, especially in the best versions of the *Prodigal Son* (Plate xxv), and Campbell Dodgson, a fine English scholar, thought him one of the world's greatest etchers. There is no doubt that between his two periods of engraving Forain had developed enormously: '. . . ses nouvelles oeuvres dans ce domain sont si éloignés des premiers qu'on ne les croirait pas de la même main . . .'.[65]

During these years Forain paid several visits to Lourdes where he also etched various scenes. In 1911 he exhibited eleven works at the International Society of Sculptors, Painters and Engravers Exhibition at the Grafton Galleries in London, and in 1912 Marcel Guérin published a Catalogue Raisonné of his etchings to date, as two years before he had compiled a catalogue of the lithographs.

The most important exhibition of Forain's works ever to be held was in that portentous year of 1913. (In 1913 also, the *Mona Lisa*, stolen in 1911, had been found and was to be returned to the Louvre.) A show comprising 409 items was organised and hung in three galleries of the Pavillon Marsan, Musée des Arts Decoratifs. Anyone who is versed in the presentation of art exhibitions knows what a temptation it is to collect together as many works as possible; they also know that the temptation should be resisted and that this number is far too large to be digested by most laymen. In this sense such an exhibition can be said to be an actual disservice, even to the greatest master. Be that as it may, Forain, now in his sixty-first year, was being presented in all his facets in an official exhibition and in a more comprehensive manner than had been possible in the Bernheim-Jeune show four years earlier.

Over a period of more than a quarter of a century, Forain's huge public had come to be so well acquainted with the work of the famous cartoonist that it could not have supposed him also to have been a painter of some stature. Now it saw, gathered under one roof, seventy oil paintings plus pastels and gouaches of his first period, together with the serious, sombre canvases of his second, an equal number of prints in etching and lithography, and finally a body of more than 270 drawings both 'straight' and satirical. Three-quarters of the exhibits had been lent by private owners, the majority of whom were well-known collectors of the last quarter of the nineteenth century.

In this exhibition Forain received the attention of the press, to a degree that would now be the envy of most artists. Four important reviews have been distilled below. Each critic agreed his genius as a biting, even devilish, satirist, his great qualities as a draughtsman, and each laid accent upon his examination of social psychology in his rôle as moralist. They gave much less attention to the painter, which is not surprising, for they had become acclimatised to the consideration of Forain as a professional journalist and not all were agile at juggling with their critical faculties. Moreover, the body of the painter's work faded almost into numerical insignificance as compared with that of the cartoonist. All but M. Paul Flat commented upon Forain's period as a 'believer'; he was also the only one who made no speculation as to what might be expected of Forain in the future.

The opinions most relevant to this book are as follows:

M. Paul Flat[66] wrote that nobody among contemporary painters was more frankly a traditionalist than Forain; that in his total artistic personality he was that great rarity, a man who had not played himself out by middle age, for there was no disproportion between the aims he had set himself and the results obtained. He thought the Dancers, by their silhouettes, their character and their flash of light upon the retina, were irresistible reminders of the celebrated Dancers of Degas; that the *Maisons Closes* in a strange way re-called those of Constantin Guys; and that before the Court scenes it was impossible not to think of Daumier. But, he warned, it would be a grave error to accuse Forain of lack of originality, for he had so well assimilated the major influences in his life that he had emerged as a new personality to join the procession of true artists.

M. René Jean[67] also made the comparison with Daumier, but he thought the two artists were of a very dissimilar wit, and that some of Forain's finest pictures—elegant and sober—were those in which his pity for all who found life implacable had been evoked. Hence his recent evolution which had surprised some people, but which was perfectly natural since this very pity had led him to the consoling nobility of Christianity. He thought Forain had been created by his period.

M. Raymond Bouyer[68] described Forain as the polemist of the pencil, more severe than the Fathers of the Church with the weaknesses of the flesh. He considered that Forain's paintings were not those of a beautiful painter in love with colour or the handling of *matière*, but he described him as the Juvénal of form and gesture who attained a grandiose emotion, an eloquence that ushered in his most recent etchings of religious compositions.

M. Henri Ghéon's review[69] is by far the most probing of the four, filling many pages of the journal, with illustrations of paintings and drawings accompanying it. At the same time as Forain's, there was also an exhibition of Japanese prints at the Musée des Arts Decoratifs, so Ghéon began his review by pointing out that the genius Hokusai, the 'old fool who loved drawing', filled the neighbouring galleries, and that his French emulator would have appreciated the delicate thought that had inspired this *rapprochement*. To Ghéon, Forain was a complex artist who continually searched for a more complete means of expression; he said that most people thought the satirist had eclipsed the artist but, in truth, the latter was greater than the former. The *Juvénal du Figaro*, despite his powerful and personal drawings, had an infinitely varied and prolific output and should not be remembered only as a mordant polemist. He tried to unravel the contradictory elements in the work of Forain, alongside whom an artist like Degas appeared simple and direct. He said that in his beginnings Forain was a painter rather than a draughtsman, for his steady progress in the latter capacity really began after 1890. The early oils, very much of the period, were delicate and subtle and strongly influenced by Manet, Degas and Morisot—excusable at that stage. But he learned to transpose, and with his excessive sensibility Forain retained until the end a tendency to reflect what most struck him as being admirable. Original or not, he was a gifted painter, who seeking his way found several between tradition and Impressionism. Without doubt he would go far. His gift of moral observation which, up till then, had constrained the painter would permit the satirical draughtsman to develop—it made him more like a writer such as Becque than a painter like Degas. His first regard was not for form but for the appearance of people, therefore in his *Foyers de Danse* Forain's intention was different from that of Degas. Degas was also ironic but he remained distant and calm; his interest could not be detracted for it was purely pictorial. Forain was nervous, curious and intense;

always the Paris street urchin who was so engrossed in the life around him that he forgot his art.

If Daumier and Forain both enjoyed the same success as journalist-draughtsmen, both suffered from misunderstanding as painters. Nothing else connected them. The painter took pride of place with Daumier, the draughtsman had gone too far for Forain the painter to be able to follow him. Ghéon then asks himself why, in one word, does the same subject lose part of its value by being transferred from the drawing-sheet to the painted canvas? He notes that there are certain exceptions, but he is making a general résumé. Forain's later pictures are sad but well painted, and they take on more éclat when the photographer reduces them to black and white, that is, to the state of drawings. In spite of their qualities as paintings they are the work of a great draughtsman. Forain, the painter, has not yet exhausted his resources.

In the year of this 1913 exhibition the art world of Paris was yet seething with activity and creation, for the old Renoir and Monet were still painting side by side with Picasso, Bonnard, Rouault and so many others, and still the scene was excitingly controversial.

Then came the outbreak of war, and for the second time in Forain's life, France was threatened by the Boche. With all the vitality and passion of a young man, '. . . son crayon devint son fusil; Forain commencait à combattre'.[70] The Christian artist became a fighter, and le Figaro, l'Opinion and other journals published his railings against the enemy and his grave concern for the sufferings of his compatriots. The war paintings were as weak as had been the canvases of the Gospel—the drawings were magnificent. How simple and telling is the *Soldat dans une Trenche* of 1914 (Plate xxii) with its broad washes superimposed by the brush loaded with black. *La Borne, Verdun, 1916* (Plate xxvi) needs no caption to convey the horror of the devastating sacrifices—it is a symbol of all frightful battles; the terrible story is there for all to see. Not only did it appear in le Figaro of March 1916, but two years later a *légende* was added—'Bis hier, Wallenstein, und nicht weiter' ('Up to here, Wallenstein, and no further'): it was reproduced as a tract and dropped in huge numbers behind the enemy lines. Forain offered the original drawing to Pétain, the defender of Verdun—a drawing that could rank with Goya's anti-war series and with Picasso's *Guernica* in the passion of its message.

Forain could not bear the seeming inactivity of remaining a civilian. Much to his pride, Jean-Loup was already with his regiment at Rheims, and at the age of sixty-two, Forain was also determined to enlist. Somehow or other he managed to enrol as a camouflage artist and was put in charge of concealing the viaduct at Chantilly. In 1917, having been quite content to join up as an ordinary private, Forain was promoted to the rank of second lieutenant. Pétain himself wrote a letter of confirmation: 'Vous êtes Sous-lieutenant, grade, mon cher Forain, dont vous serez le doyen',[71] and it is more than likely that he had used his influence with regard to the artist's promotion.

For some time Forain had been able to count the then-General Pétain among his apparently small circle of friends. A bond of sympathy and mutual respect existed between these two men of such varying professions whose only common denominator would appear to have been the overwhelming love each had for his country. Again, no account of their meeting seems traceable. Forain sometimes went to stay at Pétain's home at Villeneuve-Loubet and once when M. Edmond de Rothschild, with whom he had been dining, gave him two bottles of the wine he had enjoyed at their table he kept one to take as a gift to Pétain. Forain was careful to point out that it was a Chateau-Latour of 1870—a precious gift from a man who was fond of 'good food and sharp talk'. On one occasion the *Maréchal* visited Forain when he was ill in bed (the date is not given but it must have been well towards the end of the artist's life), and he invited Forain to go and stay with him. Pétain sat by the bedside holding Forain's hand for a long while, a gesture which deeply touched the latter. 'Monsieur, le maréchal, je suis tout à fait honoré d'aller chez vous; mais ce que me touche au plus profond de ma coeur, c'est votre amitié.'[72] When they were alone Forain told Jeanne that although he had met many interesting people during his life he had never before known friendship.

It is impossible to imagine the strength of fury that Marshal Pétain's terrible fate would have aroused in Forain. The great soldier who had devoted the entirety of his very long life to the service of his country, who, because of his public esteem, had been persuaded out of retirement in his middle eighties to become Chief of State when France was under German occupation, was finally branded à traitor—and no Zola was forthcoming. There can be no doubt whatsoever that Forain would not have taken the same stance that he did over the Dreyfus affair. Pétain died in prison, and justice to his memory has still not been done.

From the time of their first meeting right up until the end of his life, Degas was never far from Forain's thoughts and, famed reparteeist as he was himself, Forain tremendously appreciated the dry witticisms of the older man and in conversation was continually quoting them. Even more he treasured Degas' approbation. The latter's house in the rue Victor Massé, which Sickert had called 'the lighthouse of my existence',[73] was to be demolished and after a quarter of a century of tenancy Degas, then seventy-eight, had had to uproot himself. Completely disorientated in his new home, ill and practically blind, he would wander about the empty streets of Paris just after dawn like, as Forain described him, an old lion with a white mane.[74] After his enrolment Forain met him on one of these meanders and greeted him. Degas recognised the thin, rasping voice—'. . . il me tâte et il touche mes boutons d'uniform . . . "Alors," il me dit, "Monsieur, c'est honorable!"'.[75]

Three months before Armistice day a shell from 'Big Bertha', one of the long-range German guns bombarding Paris, fell upon Barbidienne's bronze foundry. 'C'est ça qui va faire des Rodin!'[76] was Forain's disparaging remark; '. . . Rodin ira diminuant comme Besnard'[77] was another—and these of a man who, today, is generally acclaimed as probably the greatest sculptor since Michelangelo! But here Forain was far from alone, for many artists during the course of history have made equally mistaken assessments of their contemporaries and these amusing erroneous forecasts have now become legendary.

It seems that Forain was able to observe all the aspects of war including combat in the trenches so, from a camouflage artist, he became what would today be known as a war correspondent. In this capacity he continued to send drawings to his papers. Among the final ones were protests against the Conference of Paris of 1919 and the ensuing Treaty of Versailles whose terms he denounced as being too lenient towards Germany and a sacrifice of France's interests in favour of international considerations. Forain's last war drawing was published in July 1919; it showed M. Clemenceau surrounded by ambassadors at a long table in the Palace of Versailles and under it was a particularly bitter comment.

In 1920, Mr Mayer, a director of Colnaghi's, called at the rue Spontini and was received 'de façon exquise'. The purpose of the visit was to offer Forain an exhibition in Colnaghi's London gallery; forty canvases were needed out of which the sale of ten would be guaranteed. Knowing that the director was of

German origin, though since a naturalised Englishman, Forain showed his war pictures and with much mirth made many sarcastic remarks ridiculing the German people. But his insensitive jests fell flat indeed, for Mr Mayer laughed louder and longer than Forain himself. Forain, for once, had met his match. The exhibition of paintings did not take place; Forain thought that the English would not understand or appreciate them and he therefore refused to make any prices for Mr Mayer. But this was not the only reason, for a similar project had been put to him during the previous year and he had then parried by saying that his drawings could go to London but not his paintings as he was nervous of their being damaged in transit. Mme Forain was of the opinion that her husband could not face all the work that the arrangements and formalities of such an exhibition would entail; moreover it would deprive him of much precious working time. Mr Mayer did not, however, leave the studio empty-handed, for he managed to buy a large number of drawings and prints. He had wanted the entire series of etchings, but by the time they got on to the subject the visit had lasted for more than two hours; Forain was exhausted and closed the matter by saying that he would discuss it with M. Gimpel. Forain, like many painters, was often loath to part with his work. As far as his paintings were concerned they never quite satisfied him and, understandably, he did not want to let them out into the world. To his wife's despair it frequently happened that a canvas that she had admired one evening became quite unrecognisable by the following day because her husband had either overworked it—usually to its detriment—or over-painted it with another subject. After a while Mme Forain learned prudence and, recognising Forain's innate contrariness, wisely refrained from any expressions of approval.

Over the years Forain had been made successively a Chevalier, Officier and finally a Commandeur de la Légion d'honneur and, like all good Frenchmen, he wore his red rosette with tremendous pride. He had been elected President of the Société Nationale des Beaux-Arts and was acting as a kind of travelling Ambassador of the Arts for France. Just as Sickert, despite his love of the unconventional, had so valued his own late election to the Royal Academy of London that he added the letters A.R.A. to his signature even on his early paintings, so Forain too adored his official recognition. The greatest prize of all had so far, however, eluded him. Since 1911 his name had been put forward as a candidate, but he had to wait a further twelve long years until, upon the vacancy created by the death of Léon Bonnat, he succeeded that painter as a member of the Institut de France and had the right to wear the famous sword. But 'quelles que fussent devenues sa gloire et sa célébrité, Forain ne cessa jamais d'être Forain même sous l'habit vert de membre de l'Institut ... Une réplique acérée, une riposte cinglante mettaient vite dans ses yeux un éclat et dans sa voix un accent ou se melaient à sa verve chapenoise la gouaille parisienne.'[78] Sickert had enjoyed the fun of having been made an Associate of the Royal Academy; he also said that he was proud to have been recognised by an institution of which Turner had been a member. Had he not been too big a man to bother about such things he would have realised how ridiculous and unseemly it was that he was never invited to become a full Academician during the ten years that elapsed before his resignation. Forain was better treated, for—admittedly only a year before his death—he was invited to be, and became, an Honorary Academician, a custom instituted as a mark of homage to a few living foreign painters. Dunoyer de Segonzac and Bonnard were two others to accept this invitation.

Forain was deadly serious about all his official honours. A man of the 'old order', he gloried in receiving France's greatest academic distinction and appears to have considered the final winning of it a more splendid achievement than his remarkable artistic output and his unique variability. How unlike the lone master were these two disciples of Degas, Forain and Sickert. In order to ensure that his triumph should go down to posterity, Forain had himself photographed *tenant son épee d'Académicien*. A print of this is cherished by his granddaughter, Mme Jeanne Chagnaud-Forain who still lives in the family home at le Chesnay, now sadly depleted of most of its ground and hemmed in by the new township of Parly II. With a touching, and to the foreigner a somewhat puzzling, sentimentality, Forain's country retreat has been carefully kept as nearly as possible as he, and later Mme Forain, left it—an illogical phenomenon among a logical people. Yet such a paradox is frequently to be remarked in France, where it is not at all unusual to find ateliers preserved through one or two generations, with their easels, palettes, paints, chalks and finished or unfinished canvases in order or in complete disarray, according to the temperament of the painter who worked there. Distinguished or insignificant, the artist has, for a while at least, this modest shrine to his memory.

In the early twenties Forain renounced his social strictures, '... comprenant que les plus heureuses créations s'usent à la longue',[79] and in 1925 he ended his many years of collaboration with journals. One of his final satirical drawings was concerned with Poincaré's defence of the franc, *Marianne Défendant son Coffre-Fort contre les Politiciens*. His last years were spent at le Chesnay, working as far as his strength permitted and walking among the old trees that he loved, so many of which have since been felled to give way to the soulless concrete of the mid twentieth century. He was amongst his dear ones: his wife, his son—who did a dry-point of him the year before his death—and his little granddaughter. Steadily failing in health and worn out after so long and active a life but with a mind ever acute, he still exerted himself to travel and in 1930 (as already stated) he went to Barcelona and paid a final visit to Lourdes. Not only did he continue to paint his Court-Rooms and a last Self-Portrait, but also such up-to-date subjects as *le Charleston* (Plate 52), which gouache he handled with a liveliness befitting the subject. Right to the end the wit persisted and he turned against himself a satire he had published just forty years earlier:[80] 'Le coeur est régulier, les reins fonctionnent, l'estomac est excellent . . . et-le-malade-meurt-gueri!'[81]

Forain is buried in the little local churchyard of le Chesnay. Here a privileged visitor may be taken by his devoted granddaughter to stand for a moment in homage before returning on the busy highway to Paris.

The paintings of the first part of Forain's career arouse a completely different emotional response from those of the second. The *Scènes de la Vie Parisienne*, those delightful little *Cabinet* pictures, provoke a feeling of gaiety and fun, and if there is a tiny lurking sting behind them it is easily dissipated by the enjoyment that makes their high spirits so infectious. It is difficult to resist their chuckle. Admittedly the subject is seductive, for it recalls that nostalgic era so attractive to mid twentieth century eyes, the period flavour that also accounts for some of the spell cast by Boudin, Renoir, Monet and many lesser painters of the day. Nevertheless, Forain has captured the mood, and these small paintings are jewels in their own right even though they comprise semi-precious stones.

When, with the passing of the years, Forain came to look more deeply into himself and into his relationship with life, it was through his painting that his innermost thoughts and struggles were mirrored. As an employed journalist he was forced to observe all kinds of rules and limitations; even his most freely expressed satirical drawings, those published under his own aegis, were subject to the primary necessity to communicate. But at his easel he was a private operator, his own master, and as his canvases took on a more serious tenor, becoming more 'weighty' both in content and in execution, they stirred in the spectator another kind of involvement. The Court-Room themes are based on deeply affecting human situations of a nature that Forain himself had experienced. He well understood what it meant to suffer poverty and homelessness, hunger and cold, so that his pictorial disclosures were far from being those of a superficial observer. Yet the pity he was able to kindle for the sobbing woman whose husband had been committed to prison, or for the family deprived of its support and home, is rather more on the cerebral than on the emotional level. From the essentially aesthetic angle these paintings can be magnificent, but if they also tore at the heart, then they would be masterpieces. To be entirely oneself is, after all, one of the great lessons in life and the only way of living in truth. And so in art it is imperative to speak no other thoughts and with no tongue other than one's own; without this it is impossible to achieve the ultimate. Forain, as he himself confessed when writing to Huysmans about his religious work, lacked the inner imaginative spark and had to seek it elsewhere. Once this was found he could and did turn it to his own account, but the borrowing is always evident, not because of the motif, which is of relatively small importance, but because the way of seeing, having been taken from another, inevitably lacks the deepest ring of conviction.

In the realm of pure drawing, however, Forain was an original and he was tremendously appreciated by some of the greatest artists of his day. One of his most consistent admirers was that supreme draughtsman Degas who, among the fine works of art that he had bought when his finances permitted, could rarely resist buying a Forain. He kept a table especially devoted to the younger man's prints; on it they were 'lovingly piled', the latest publication on the top. Cézanne also held Forain in great esteem and on his studio walls hung many drawings from *Doux Pays*. Lautrec's respect has already been touched upon, and even Gauguin, despite his avowed dislike of caricature— and indeed Forain was never a caricaturist—owned three of his works which he took with him to Denmark on his last visit in 1848. Together with the other pictures he had collected in Paris, he left the three small Forains with his wife when he finally departed, never to return. One of these was a pastel portrait of Valéry Roumy (Plate 21), a Montmartre cabaret singer of whom Gauguin himself had made a medallion relief in wood and plaster. Forain gave his pastel of their mutual model to Gauguin—nothing more is known about their relationship.

Rouault once wrote: 'When art was for me the Promised Land (and until death it always will be) Forain, with a black and white drawing, aroused in me a gleam, an inward perception of a rare thing . . . which, after the chore of 'drawing well' in my evening class, gave me hope. . . . I lacked the means of expression; I was ignorant; but I had a secret instinct which told me that here was the living source. . . .'[82] This was the crux of the matter. As a draughtsman Forain was complete; he had what Sickert called that 'beautiful sense of measure'—as a painter it was he who needed the 'living source'. By the time he was in his thirties, Rouault had not only found but had developed the highly individual vision that was to characterise his art for the rest of his life. It was of a flavour so private that only one insignificant follower attempted to emulate it, and he was no more than a mere copyist. But Rouault fell into the trap which, in a sense, he had set for himself and which may befall any but the most vital and enquiring of painters—he became so beguiled by his own creations that he slowly descended into being little but a *pasticheur* of himself.

In the years preceding the First World War when his art was at its highest peak, Rouault, also moved by the *Comédie Humaine*, used the Daumier-Forain theme of the Courts of Justice. His powerful and sonorous oils and mixed-media paintings bear evidence of the imprint of his short period of stained-glass working, but his delight in the theatrical reveals him as a spirit closely akin to Daumier, and far removed from Forain with his particular brand of realism.

However devout Forain may have become, it was daring—if not foolhardy —of him to have attempted the Sacred theme. Of his near contemporaries only Redon, born in 1840, and Rouault, in 1871, had sometimes been able to realise in pictorial terms that elusive sense of mysticism without falling into the chasm of *kitsch*. Even these two highly personal artists were not always able to keep on the right side of the extremely sensitive borderline. Redon succeeded in the best of his hauntingly beautiful pastels and charcoal drawings, from the richness of which medium he drew to its full extent. Rouault's fervent paintings of Christ as well as his etchings and wood engravings to André Suarès' text to the Passion were, similarly, his highest accomplishment. Belief emanates from the most secret corners of the soul and is communicated to the aware through the aura of man. In art it can most nearly be imparted through the pure medium of music, sometimes through the word, but very rarely through the brush. In his endeavour, Forain's failure was an honourable and by no means isolated one.

As was said at the beginning, the purpose of this monograph is to try to show Forain in his painterly and less familiar rôle. Those who know and admire his brilliant achievement as a cartoonist will probably be surprised to find that there was this other side to his professional career. They could never have suspected that he either found the time or had the ability to scale the heights of excellence he frequently attained as a painter—they have probably never even thought about it.

The compilation of this book has not proved easy, for despite the fact that the art of the late nineteenth and early twentieth century has by now become, if anything, over chronicled and analysed, Forain, when he is mentioned at all, is mainly referred to *en passant*, as a disciple and friend of Degas. Monographs on those known to have been in his circle, and even their own books of reminiscences, are mysteriously lacking in references to him; perhaps it was his self-indulgent verbal darts that estranged him even from his intimates so that they drew a curtain of silence across the man and his doings. In fact, this is known to have been so, for Forain could not resist the pleasure of uttering a *bon mot* even at the risk of making an enemy. This far from endearing trait must have caused his sense of loneliness and an underlying melancholy brought about by the struggle between innate shyness and the satirist's irresistible habit of scoring against another. That he prized friendship is confirmed by his words to Pétain; that he was worthy of it is shown by his attendance upon Huysmans during the writer's last illness, and by his quiet generosity to those for whom he cared. Sickert, a vivid and prolific writer, must frequently have met Forain through their close connection with Degas, yet he hardly speaks of the man—as apart from the draughtsman. In one of his rare references, he talks of 'the countless men whom Forain obliged'.[83] Mme Forain has also told how, after her husband's death, she found among the stubs in his cheque book evidence of how many men he had financially helped.

In Forain's attitude there was if not an excusable, then an understandable arrogance, for he was well aware of the power he had to provoke his readers into action. For him there were also personal reactions—he termed them 'noisy'. As a result of his cartoons he received many insulting letters which, as may be believed, received violent replies. Complexity of character is not peculiar to Forain, but there are few men of whom it may be said: '. . . son temperament [est] à la fois conservateur et anarchiste'.[84]

During his lifetime, as already stated, Forain's prints were catalogued, volumes of his satirical drawings were published and innumerable articles were written about the cartoonist and his terrifying wit. The two monographs that appeared in the year of his death are mainly in the nature of casual reminiscences recounted to the authors by the artist himself when he was already an old and very sick man whose memory, by his own admission, was fast failing. These recollections, darting hither and thither, by no means always coincide, neither do those in the third book on Forain written in 1952 in collaboration with his widow. In all three volumes dates and facts, where given, have to be accepted with reservation and pieced together with caution. If any reasons are here required for possible errors in the dating of pictures and gaps in the story of Forain, they are that research has proved frustratingly unrewarding and that revealing documents, if they do exist, have not on this occasion been made available. That references to Degas should appear so frequently seems inevitable, for he hovers around Forain like some *bon génie*—first as master, then as the precious friend, and always as a touchstone.

Should criticisms appear unnecessarily severe it need hardly be said that they are meant, not to belittle the artist, but rather to pay him the compliment of the impartiality that his achievements demand. It is hoped that this monograph may add a small word to the long history of Western art and that it may also be regarded as a tribute to the struggles, successes and failures of a very extraordinary artist and man.

NOTES TO THE TEXT

(All translations are by the Author)

1 Léandre Vaillat, *En Ecoutant Forain* (Paris, 1931), p. 7.
2 *Journal d'Edmond et Jules de Goncourt* (25 March 1882). 'This Forain has a language absolutely Parisian, made up of untranslatable expressions in whatever idiom and which, by an infinitely delicate irony, conceal the sublime.'
3 Jacques-Emile Blanche, 'Forain et Whistler', *La Renaissance Latine* (1905), p. 412.
4 Vaillat, op. cit., p. 206. 'At that age one did not pay attention as to whether a man was Jewish or not. Anti-Semitism is something that one discovers later.'
5 Jacques-Emile Blanche, 'Jean-Louis Forain: Le champénois', *Revue Hebdomadaire* (26 September 1931), p. 402. 'Forain went to bed in a rage and got up after a disturbed sleep in a greater rage, not wishing to go into the legal side of the trial, resolved not to discuss it.'
6 Jean Puget, *La Vie Extraordinaire de Forain* (Paris, 1957), p. 22. '. . . for the good of all, I denounce'.
7 Ibid., p. 124. 'The Impressionists have discovered the way to paint light, a magnificent discovery: But the cloud is also splendid, as are all the tones of a *grisaille*.'
8 René Gimpel, *Journal d'un Collectionneur-Marchand de Tableaux* (Paris, 1963), p. 150.
9 Vaillat, op. cit., p. 86. 'At the blackboard he performed wonders with chalk.'
10 Ibid., p. 83. '. . . in front of the Cathedral that I saw drawing for the first time'.
11 Charles Kunstler, *Forain*, Maîtres de l'art moderne (Paris, 1931), p. 12. 'the principles of my art'. 'Later, later, when you are able to paint . . .'
12 Ibid., p. 13. 'This is not bad . . . not bad at all . . . there are certain errors. Wait!' 'Come and see me at the studio one of these mornings.' 'Do you know that your bas-relief is splendid? . . . Only, you won't be able to do that again for thirty years. It is well understood; in the meantime you must study.'
13 Ibid., p. 14. 'Monsieur, I cannot'.
14 Ibid., p. 14. 'The precise resemblance of the features in the faces'.
15 Ibid., p. 14. 'My father cursed me, or almost, and there I was on the streets of Paris.'
16 This was when the nickname 'Gavroche' was given to Forain, after the *gamin* in Victor Hugo's *Les Miserables*.
17 Vaillat, op. cit., p. 100. 'One could hear the gunfire coming from Saint-Cloud and from Bellevue. It was like flashes of lightning on the horizon.'
18 R. H. Wilenski, *Modern French Painters* (London, 1940), p. 30. 'Come, great spirit, we await you, we want you.'
19 Enid Starkie, *Arthur Rimbaud* (London, 1947), p. 164.
20 Vaillat, op. cit., p. 101. 'It is Saturday evening and I would like to shake your hand and talk with you. . . . What has happened to the time, thirteen years ago, when Rimbaud and I waited for you in a little café in the rue Drouot, smoking our clay pipes which we moistened with many a bitter-curaco.'
21 Gimpel, op. cit., p. 343. 'I lived with him for two months . . . in an appalling hovel; it suited him, it pleased him, he was so dirty. We had only one bed; he slept on the springs and I on the mattress on the floor. . . . Life with Rimbaud was not possible, because he was a formidable drinker of absinthe. Verlaine came to fetch him, and both despised me because I would not go with them. That was the whole of their vice. People have talked about a homosexual relationship. No, I have never seen anything, I don't believe it at all. . . .'
22 Puget, op. cit., p. 28. ' ". . . your type of love disgusts me . . . You talk of an ideal, of communion of spirits: . . ." (and here an unrepeatable word)'.

23 Ibid., p. 25. 'When I am with the little dark cat I am good, for the little dark cat is very kind. When I am with the little fair cat, I am bad, for the little fair cat is ferocious.'

24 Bibliothèque Nationale, 'J.-L. Forain ... Exposition organisée pour le Centenaire de sa Naissance', Catalogue, p. 22, no. 61. '... it was a marvel, terrible and true'.

25 Ibid., p. 41, no. 203. 'I have to do some drawings for *la République des lettres*. I need a text. Find me some poems in prose. Something Parisian of course. ... With your mercilessness that should do very well. ...'

26 J. K. Huysmans, *L'Art Moderne* (Paris, 1883), p. 73. '... Here, nothing; the Independents are decidedly the only ones who can express, or at least try to express, the Parisienne and the prostitute. There is more elegance, more modernity, in the slightest sketch of a woman by L. Forain than in all the canvases of Bouveret and other manufacturers of a false world: ... they are little miracles of Parisian and elegant reality.'

27 Robert Baldick, *The Life of J. K. Huysmans* (Oxford, 1955), p. 60.

28 Huysmans, op cit., p. 105.

29 John Rewald, *Post Impressionism from Van Gogh to Gauguin* (New York, 1956), p. 497.

30 Bibliothèque Nationale Catalogue, op. cit., p. 22, no. 65. 'The numerous scenes of dancers that he gave at first to this journal seem to be a homage to his master Degas.'

31 Osbert Sitwell, editor, *A Free House! The Writing of Walter Richard Sickert* (London, 1947), p. XXIV.

32 Lamberto Vitale, 'Un fotografo fin de siesta', *le Conte Primoli* (Turin, n.d.). '... [one] finds at Florian the joyous Forain all in white flannel. He presented to me his pretty companion ...' 'She is so adorably pretty that we are present at the triumph to her beauty.... The men contemplate her in silence, the women discuss her charms in the soft Venetian language ...'

33 Bibliothèque Nationale Catalogue, op. cit., no. 209. 'I am certain that this has not bothered you very much, but I ... I stop myself because I was going to write you a love letter but you are too mocking for me to dare to betray myself ...'

34 *Journal d'Edmond de Goncourt* (7 February 1892). '... and a *croute*, if you please, on which she paints flowers with the yolk of an egg, and leaves with I don't know what: artistic pastry'.

35 *Studio Magazine* (London, August 1897).

36 William Rothenstein, *Men and Memories: 1872–1900* (London, 1931), Vol. I, pp. 40–1. Henri Gervex, *Souvenirs,* compiled Jules Bertaut (Paris, 1924), p. 60.

37 In the company of Mme Jeanne Chagnaud-Forain, the artist's granddaughter, M. St Laurent kindly showed me around his *maison*.

38 Bibliothèque Nationale Catalogue, op. cit., pp. 12–13. 'Record everyday life, to show the ridiculousness of certain sorrows, the sadness of many joys, and to state, sometimes harshly, by what hypocritical means life tends to manifest itself in us. ...'

39 Vaillat, op. cit., p. 207. '... he [Forain] went to London to be present at the centenary of the permission granted to Catholics to celebrate Mass in England'.

40 'A personal account of Degas by Sickert', *Burlington Magazine* (December 1917). ' "Monsieur Degas, in England the gentleman is always clean shaven." "Monsieur Forain, in France it is exactly the opposite. In France it is only the servants who shave." '

41 Puget, op. cit., opp. p. 32.

42 Vaillat, op. cit., p. 72. '... so that there should be at least one Frenchman at the Hansi trial'.

43 Ibid., p. 182. '... I have always been mad about novelties. I wanted to have the first bicycle, the first tandem, the first automobile'.

44 Kunstler, op. cit., p. 21. '... rich women and snobs infatuated with painting, music and literature. ...'

45 Henry Zerner, Introduction, 'James Jacques Joseph Tissot', Exhibition Catalogue, Museum of Art, Rhode Island School of Design (Providence, USA, 1968).

46 Jacques-Emile Blanche, *Portraits of a Lifetime (1870–1914)* (London, 1937), p. 156.

47 Jean Lapeyre, Introduction, Paul Helleu Exhibition Catalogue, Musée de Dieppe (1962), p. VII. 'England is magnificent, splendid, imposing . . .'

48 Ibid., p. III. 'Ugliness filled him with a kind of frightening and astonished horror.'

49 René Gimpel, op. cit., p. 71. 'He is the ghost of a Watteau'.

50 Dario Cecchi, *Boldini* (Turin, 1962), note to p. 151 (Cf. Piero Romanelli, 'Degas', *Figaro*, 13 March 1937). 'My dear Boldini, what a great talent you have, but what a strange idea you have of humanity: when you paint a man you make him ridiculous; and when you paint a woman, you dishonour her!'

51 J. P. Crespelle, *Les Maîtres de la Belle Epoque* (Paris, 1966), p. 150. 'The quality of Steinlen's art was not, unfortunately, equal to his sentiments . . .'

52 Jean Adhémar, *Honoré Daumier* (Paris, 1954), p. 84 and note to p. 92. '. . . Daumier once again became the Master of caricaturists. Forain, Willette, among others still considered him their God'.

53 Reference to Balzac's *Illusions perdues*.

54 Adhémar, op. cit., p. 61. 'I wanted to say that the satirical genius of Daumier had nothing to do with satanical genius. . . .'

55 Ibid., p. 33. 'A man who abuses the public's credulity'.

56 Baldick, op. cit., p. 106.

57 Ibid., p. 288 (Letter to Brousolle).

58 Ibid, p. 349.

59 Ibid., p. 201 ('En Route').

60 Gimpel, op. cit., pp. 162-3. '. . . my piety came from having lived at the foot of the Cathedral. I was five or six years old. . . . Towards the age of eighteen, life called. . . . This folly lasted until I was about thirty-five; then faith came to me at one fell swoop and it has done nothing else but grow.'

61 Baldick, op. cit., p. 180 (Havelock Ellis).

62 Bibliothèque Nationale Catalogue, op. cit., p. 43, no. 215. 'comforted and ready for more worthy works of art . . . all that I have done up to now in art seems to me to be fruitless and I feel that I shall never have any rest until I have confessed and manifested my Faith through the means that God has given me. . . .'

63 Vaillat, op. cit., pp. 192-3. 'You may certainly believe one thing, and that is that if God has brought you back to him as he has me, it is so that we might be useful to him according to the extent of our poor forces. He will give you the means as he has given them to me.'

64 Daniel Halévy, *My Friend Degas* (London, 1966), p. 120.

65 Adhémar and Léthève, 'Inventaire du Fonds Francais', *XIX Siècle*, 8. '. . . his new works in this field are so far removed from the first that one would not believe them to be by the same hand. . . .'

66 Paul Flat, 'Un grand satiriste social—J. L. Forain', *Revue politique et littéraire* (15 February 1913).

67 René Jean, 'Exposition de J. L. Forain, Musée des Arts Decoratifs', *La Chronique des Arts et de la Curiosité* (January 1913).

68 Raymond Bouyer, 'Jean-Louis Forain', *Le Bulletin de l'Art ancien et moderne* (January 1913).

69 Henri Ghéon, 'Jean-Louis Forain', *Art et Decoration* (January 1913).

70 Puget, op. cit., p. 97. '. . . his pencil became his gun; Forain started to fight'.

71 Ibid., p. 99. 'You have been given the rank of second lieutenant, my dear Forain, and you will be the doyen'.

72 Vaillat, op. cit., pp. 34-5. 'I shall be much honoured to visit you; but what touches me to the depth of my heart is your friendship.'

73 Lillian Browse, *Sickert* (London, 1960), p. 26.

74 Vaillat, op. cit., p. 131.

75 Ibid., p. 132. '. . . he felt me, and he touched the buttons of my uniform. . . . "Well, Monsieur, this is honourable!" he said.'

76 Gimpel, op. cit., p. 64. 'That is how Rodins are made!'

77 Ibid, p. 246. 'Rodin will fall off like Besnard'.

78 Bibliothèque Nationale Catalogue, op. cit., p. 45, no. 229. 'whatever glory and celebrity he might have attained, Forain never ceased to be Forain, even when he was wearing the green dress-coat of the Institute. . . . A sharp reply, a lashing repartee quickly brought a glitter to his eyes and to his voice an accent that was a mixture of Champenois breeziness and Parisian banter.'

79 Puget, op. cit., p. 127. '. . . understanding that the best creations eventually wear thin'.

80 Jacqueline Magne, 'Forain témoin de son temps: la satire sociale et morale', *Gazette des Beaux-Arts* (April 1973), p. 242 (Cf. *Figaro*, 10 January 1891).

81 Puget, op. cit., p. 139. 'The heart is regular, the kidneys function, the stomach is excellent . . . and the patient dies cured!'

82 James Thrall Thoby, Preface, 'George Rouault: Paintings and prints', Exhibition Catalogue, Museum of Modern Art, (New York, 1945).

83 Sitwell, op. cit., p. 254.

84 Adhémar and Léthève, op. cit. '. . . his temperament is, at the same time, that of a conservative and an anarchist'.

Notes on some Names mentioned in Text

BECQUE, HENRI (1837–1899), French dramatist; born Paris.

BÉSNARD, PAUL-ALBERT (1849–1934), French painter; born Paris.

BONNAT, LÉON-JOSEPH (1834–1923), French painter; born Bayonne.

CARAN D'ACHE—nom de plume of Emmanuel Poiré (1858–1909), French caricaturist; born Moscow. *Caran d'Ache* is Russian for 'pencil'.

CARPEAUX, JEAN-BAPTISTE (*c.* 1827–1875), French sculptor; born Valenciennes.

DODGSON, CAMPBELL (1867–1948), appointed to the Print Room at the British Museum 1893; Keeper from 1912–1932.

GILL, ANDRÉ—real name Gosset de Guines (1840–1885), French cartoonist; born Paris.

HALÉVY, LUDOVIC (1834–1908), French writer; born Paris.

HANSI—nom de plume of Jean-Jacques Waltz (1873–1951), Alsatian caricaturist; born Colmar.

JACQUESSON DE LA CHEVREUSE, LOUIS-MARIE FRANÇOIS (1839–1903), French painter; born Toulouse.

JUVÉNAL (*c.* 65–128), satirical Latin poet; born Aquinum.

LEWIS-BROWN, JOHN (1829–1980), French painter, mainly *animalier*; born Bordeaux.

LEYS, HENRI JAN-AUGUSTYN (1815–1869), Belgian painter, born Antwerp.

MARTELLI, DIÉGO (1839–1896), Italian art critic; born Florence.

MOREAU, GUSTAVE (1826–1898), French painter; born Paris.

PAGANS, tenor and guitarist.

PELLEGRINI, CARLO (1839–1889), Italian cartoonist; born Capua.

PRINCETEAU, RENÉ (*c.* 1844–1914), French painter, mainly *animalier*; born Libourne.

RUDE, FRANÇOIS (1784–1855), French sculptor; born Dijon.

SARGENT, JOHN SINGER (1856–1925), British painter; born Florence.

SEM—nom de plume of Goursat (1863–1934), French cartoonist; born Perigueux.

SIEBURG, FRIEDRICH (b. 1893), German writer; author of *Gott in Frankreich*.

STEVENS, ALFRED (1823–1906), Belgian painter; born Brussels.

WILLETTE, ADOLPHE (1857–1926), French painter and draughtsman; born Châlons-sur-Marne.

SELECT BIBLIOGRAPHY

Adhémar, Jean, *Honoré Daumier* (Paris, 1954).
Adhémar, Jean and Léthève, Jacques, 'Inventaire du fonds français', *XIX Siècle*, 8.
Baldick, Robert, *The Life of J. K. Huysmans* (Oxford, 1955).
    The Goncourts (London, 1960).
    The Siege of Paris (London, 1965).
Bergerat, Emile, 'Souvenirs d'un enfant de Paris', *Comoedia* (Paris, 11 December 1912).
Bibliothèque Nationale, Paris, 'J.-L. Forain', Exhibition Catalogue (1952).
Blanche, Jacques-Emile, 'Forain et Whistler', *La Renaissance Latine* (Paris, 1905).
    'Jean-Louis Forain', *La Renaissance Latine* (1907).
    'Jean-Louis Forain: le champénois', *Revue Hebdomadaire* (Paris, 26 September 1931).
    Portraits of a Lifetime (1870–1914) (London, 1937).
    More Portraits of a Lifetime (London, 1939).
Bodelsen, Merete, 'Gauguin studies', *Burlington Magazine* (April, 1967).
    Gauguin og Impressionisterne (Copenhagen, 1968).
    'Gauguin the collector', *Burlington Magazine* (September 1970; part translation of 1968 book).
Bouyer, Raymond, 'Jean-Louis Forain', *le Bulletin de l'Art ancien et moderne* (Paris, January 1913).
Brisson, Adolphe, *Nos humoristes. Jean-Louis Forain* (Paris, 1900).
Browse, Lillian, *Sickert* (London, 1960).
Bucarelli, Palma, and Caradente, Giovanni, 'La Mostra dei Macchiaioli', Exhibition Catalogue (Rome, 1956).
Cecchi, Dario, *Boldini* (Turin, 1962).
Colette, *My Apprenticeships and Music-Hall Sidelights* (London, 1967).
    The Rainy Moon—the Kepi (London, 1975).
Crespelle, J. P., *Les Maîtres de la Belle Epoque* (Paris, 1966).
Daudet, Alphonse, Preface, *Album de Forain* (Paris, 1893).
Daudet, Léon, *Salons et Journaux* (Paris, 1932).
Davis, Frank, 'Talking about Forain', *Illustrated London News* (5 December 1959).
de Goncourt, Edmond, *Journal* (Paris, 1895), Tome IX.
de Leiris, Alain, Preface, Steinlen Exhibition Catalogue, Charles Slatkin Gallery, (New York, 1963).
de Logu, Giuseppe, editor, *Pittura Italiana dell' Ottocento* (Bergamo, 1955).
de Montesquiou, Robert, *Helleu—Peintre et Graveur* (Paris, 1913).
de Nittis, Giuseppe, *Notes et Souvenirs* (Paris, 1895).
Dodgson, Campbell, 'Forain; Draughtsman, Lithographer, Etcher', Exhibition Catalogue, (New York, 1936).
Dortu, M. B., Preface, 'Chevaux et Cavaliers—René Princeteau', Exhibition Catalogue, Galerie Schmit (Paris, 1965).
Durand-Ruel, Paul, Archives, Paris.
Flat, Paul, 'Un grand satiriste social—J. L. Forain,' *Revue politique et littéraire* (Paris, 15 February 1913).
Frantz, Henri, 'J.-L. Forain: peintre, dessinateur et lithographe', *Le Figaro Illustré* (Paris, February 1902).
Geoffroy, Gustave, 'Forain', *Numero special de l'Art et les Artistes* (Paris, November 1921).

Gervex, Henri, *Souvenirs*, compiled Jules Bertaut (Paris, 1924).

Ghéon, Henri, 'Jean-Louis Forain', *Art et Decoration* (January, 1913).

Gillet, Louis, 'Forain, son exposition aux arts decoratifs', *Revue Hebdomadaire* (Paris, 23 January 1913).

Gimpel, René, *Journal d'un Collectionneur-Marchand de Tableaux* (Paris, 1963).

Guérin, Marcel, *J.-L. Forain lithographe, Catalogue Raisonné* (Paris, 1910).

J.-L. Forain aquafortiste, Catalogue Raisonné (Paris, 1912), 2 vols.

Halévy, Daniel, *My Friend Degas* (London, 1966).

Heintzelman, Arthur, Preface, Jean-Louis Forain Exhibition Catalogue, Museum of Fine Arts (Springfield, Mass., 1956).

Huysmans, J. K., *Croquis Parisiens—Eaux-fortes de Forain* (Paris, 1880).

L'Art Moderne (Paris, 1883).

Jean, René, 'Exposition de J.-L. Forain, Musée des Arts Decoratifs', *La Chronique des Arts et de la Curiosité* (Paris, January 1913).

Kunstler, Charles, *Forain*, Maîtres de l'Art Moderne (Paris, 1931).

Lapeyre, Jean, Preface, Paul Helleu Exhibition Catalogue, Musée de Dieppe (1962).

Lassaigne, Jacques, *Lautrec*, Le Gout de Notre Temps (Paris, 1953).

Laver, James, *The First Decadent—Life of Huysmans* (London, 1954).

Léon, Paul, and Vallery-Radot, Jean, *see* Bibliothèque Nationale Catalogue (1952).

Mack, Gerstle, *Toulouse-Lautrec* (London, 1938).

Magne, Jacqueline, 'Forain témoin de son temps: la satire sociale et morale', extract from thesis in *Gazette des Beaux-Arts* (Paris, April 1973).

Maison, K. E., *Honoré Daumier, Catalogue Raisonné* (London, 1968), 2 vols.

Ojetti, Ugo, *La Pittura Italiana Dell'otto Cento* (Milan-Rome, 1929).

Puget, Jean, *La Vie Extraordinaire de Forain* (Paris, 1957).

Rebatet, Marguerite, *Degas* (Paris, 1944).

Renoir, Jean, *Renoir, my Father* (London, 1962).

Rewald, John, *Post Impressionism from Van Gogh to Gauguin* (New York, 1956).

Rothenstein, William, *Men and Memories: 1872–1900* (London, 1931), Vol. 1.

Salaman, M. C., 'Modern Masters of Etching', *Studio Magazine* (1925).

Sitwell, Osbert, *A Free House! The Writing of Walter Richard Sickert* (London, 1947).

Starkie, Enid, *Arthur Rimbaud* (London, 1947).

Talmeyr, Maurice, Preface, *Album Forain* (Paris, 1896).

Thévoz, Michel, Preface, 'Théophile-Alexandre Steinlen', Retrospective Exhibition Catalogue, (Charleroi, Lausanne and Basle, 1970–1).

Thoby, James Thrall, Preface, 'Georges Rouault: paintings and prints', Exhibition Catalogue, Museum of Modern Art (New York, 1945).

Vaillat, Léandre, *En Ecoutant Forain* (Paris, 1931).

Vaudoyer, J. L., *L'Echo de Paris* (13 July 1931).

Vauxcelles, Louis, Preface, Forain Exhibition Catalogue, Galerie Raphaël Gérard (Paris, 1937).

Venturi, Lionello, *Les archives de l'Impressionnisme*, Exhibition Catalogue (Paris and New York, 1939).

Vollard, Ambroise, *Souvenirs d'un Marchand de Tableaux* (Paris, 1937).

Walker, Murray, 'Jean-Louis Forain—a reassessment', *Art Bulletin of Victoria* (Melbourne, 1968–9).

Wasell, Nancy Michelle, 'Jean-Louis Forain, the Painter', thesis submitted to the Faculty of the University of North Carolina (1969).

Wilenski, R. H., *Modern French Painters* (London, 1940).

Zerner, Henri, and Brooke, David S., Preface, 'James Jacques Joseph Tissot', Retrospective Exhibition Catalogue, (Providence and Toronto, 1968).

Zillhardt, Madeleine, *Louise-Catherine Breslau et ses Amis* (Paris, 1932).

PRINCIPAL EXHIBITIONS
OF THE WORK OF FORAIN

1890   Galerie Boussod-Valadon, Paris: 'Forain' (drawings).
1909   Galerie Bernheim-Jeune, Paris: 'Forain' (all media).
1911   International Society of Sculptors, Painters and Gravers, London (all media).
1913   Musée des Arts Decoratifs, Paris: 'Forain' (the most important one-man exhibition).
1921   Chambre Syndicale des Beaux Arts, Paris (Forain and Mme Jeanne Forain).
1923   Salon de la Société Nationale des Beaux-Arts, Paris.
1931   Galerie d'Art du Théâtre Pigalle, Paris.
1933   Amigos del Arte, Buenos-Aires.
1935   Arthur Tooth and Sons, London: 'Forain'.
1937   Galerie Raphaël Gérard, Paris: 'Forain'.
1945   Salon de la Société Nationale des Beaux-Arts, Paris: 'Forain'.
1950   Cultural Division of the French Embassy, New York: 'Forain' (prints).
1951   Galerie Beaugin, Paris: 'Forain' (paintings).
1952   Bibliothèque Nationale, Paris: 'Forain' (the most comprehensive exhibition and informative catalogue).
1956   Museum of Fine Arts, Springfield, Mass: 'Forain' (paintings).
1964   Roland, Browse and Delbanco, London: 'Forain' (paintings and drawings).
1964   Galerie Reichenbach, Paris: 'Forain' (paintings).
1965   Galerie Reichenbach, Paris: 'Forain' (paintings).
1967   Hirschl and Adler Gallery, New York: 'Forain' (paintings).

WORKS EXHIBITED BY FORAIN
IN THE IMPRESSIONIST EXHIBITIONS

4e *Exposition de Peinture* 28 avenue de l'Opéra, Paris. 10 April–11 May 1879.

Peinture
82   Portrait de M.M. . . .

Aquarelles (most of these are what we now qualify as 'gouaches')
83   Portrait de M. Coquelin Cadet dans le Sphinx.
84   Portrait de M. H. . . . (perhaps M. Huysmans).
85   Portrait de M. H. . . . (perhaps M. Huysmans).
86   Intérieur de café (*appartient à* M. Cheramy).
87   Fin de souper (*appartient à* M. Doucet).
88   Loge d'actrice (*appartient à* M. Hecht).
89   Sortie de théâtre (*appartient à* Mme H. Lamy).

90   Pourtour des Folies Bergère (*appartient à* M. May).
91   Pourtour des Folies Bergère (*appartient à* M. Félix Bouchor).
92   Pourtour des Folies Bergère (*appartient à* M. Hecht).
93   Entr'acte (*appartient à* M. Jouron).
94   Coulisses de théâtre (*appartient à* M. Hecht).
95   Coulisses de théâtre (*appartient à* M. Huysmans).
96   Café d'acteurs (*appartient à* M. Hecht).
97   Femme au café (*appartient à* Mme Martin).
98   Coin de salon (*appartient à* Mme G. C. . . .).
99   Cabotin en demi-deuil (*appartient à* M. Coquelin).
100   Pourtour des Folies Bergère (*appartient à* M. Coquelin Cadet).
101   Un éventail (*appartient à* Mme Martin).
102   Un éventail (*appartient à* Mme Martin).
103   Un éventail (*appartient à* Mme Martin).
104   Un éventail (*appartient à* M. Angelo).
105   Un écran (*appartient à* M. Alphonse Daudet).
106   Un écran (*appartient à* M. Alphonse Daudet).
107   Un dessin (*appartient à* M. Léon Hennique).

5e *Exposition de Peinture* 10 rue des Pyramids, Paris. 1–30 April, 1880.

Maison close.
La Promenade du voyou à la Campagne (illustration to Verlaine's poem).
Actrice allant rentrer en scène (*appartient à* Mlle V. de M.).
Etude d'homme.
Six dessins.
Deux Eau fortes.

6e *Exposition de Peinture* 35 boulevard des Capucines, Paris. 2 April–1 May 1881.

20   Au théâtre—*peinture*.
21   Coin de Bal masqué à l'Opéra—*peinture*.
22   Loge d'actrice—*aquarelle* (*appartient à* M. E. Blum).
23   Couloir de théâtre—*aquarelle* (*appartient à* M. A. Meyer).
24   Marine—*aquarelle*.
25   Portrait de Mlle Madeleine C. . . .—*pastel*.
26   Dessin.
27   Dessin.
28   Dessin.
29   Dessin.

8e *Exposition de Peinture* 1 rue Laffitte, Paris. 15 May–15 June 1886.

29   Femme à sa toilette (*appartient à* M. Durand-Ruel).
30   Place de la Concorde (*appartient à* M. Meunier).
31   Portrait de Mme W.
32   Portrait de Mme S.
33   Femme respirant des fleurs (*appartient à* M. Durand-Ruel).
34   Femme fumant une cigarette (*appartient à* Mme T.).
35   Tête d'étude.
36   Tête d'étude.
37   Jeune fille au bal (*appartient à* Mme de P.).
38   Femme en noir (*appartient à* M. le Comte de F.).
39   Souvenir de Chantilly—*esquisse en grisaille* (*appartient à* Mme S.).
40   Un coin a l'Opéra—*dessin à l'encre de chine* (*appartient à* M. Donnadille).
41   Pompier dans les coulisses de l'Opéra.

COLOUR
PLATES

NOTES ON THE COLOUR PLATES

Frontispiece LE CLIENT *or* MAISON CLOSE

Gouache; 9¾ × 12¾ in. (25 × 32.5 cm); signed upper right *Louis Forain* and dated 1878.

Exhibited: Fifth Impressionist Exhibition (L'Exposition des Indépendants), Paris, 1880, as *Maison close*.

Literature: Huysmans, *L'Art Moderne*, (Paris, 1883), page 107.

Provenance: Rauch, Geneva, 13–15 June 1960/Reid and Lefevre, London.

In the possession of a private collector, London.

This must be one of the wittiest and gaiest brothel scenes in the whole pictorial history of the *maisons closes*—a statement which could only be made with ease against the background of the 1970s when but a tiny minority might bat an eyelid against free love, prostitution, or male and female nudity: in fact, at a time when sex, verbally or visually, has become a veritable bore.
Prostitution, in France, did not come out into the open until a hundred years ago when Huysmans and Edmond de Goncourt published, almost simultaneously, their books on the life of a prostitute. It is therefore not surprising that Huysmans, in his *L'Art Moderne*, wrote with a mingling of sadness and disgust of the protagonists of Forain's *Maisons Closes,* together with admiration for the artist who 'est l'un des peintres de la vie moderne les plus incisifs que je connaisse'.

I LA RENCONTRE AU FOYER *or* ENTRE-ACTE

Gouache; 13½ × 8½ in. (34.3 × 21.6 cm); signed lower right *Ls Forain*; 1877.

Exhibited: perhaps the *Couloir de Théâtre* in the Sixth Impressionist Exhibition, 1881, No. 23, *appartient à* M. A. Meyer.

Provenance: Reichenbach, Paris, as *Entre-Acte*/Roland, Browse and Delbanco, London, 1965/the Hon. Mrs Pleydell-Bouverie, London, 1965/Sothebys, Pleydell-Bouverie Executors' sale as *La Rencontre au Foyer*, 3 July 1968/Marlborough Galleries, London.

Collection: the Hon. Mrs Pleydell Bouverie.

In the possession of a private collector, London.

Degas was a strikingly brilliant composer who knew exactly where the edge of the canvas should cut his figures. This device contributed towards one of his aims, to capture the casual, the unself-conscious effect. At a very early date Forain, too, showed his natural aptitude for composition; he also showed that he had learned the 'cutting' lesson from Degas. He was right at the beginning of his career—his first satirical drawing had been accepted for publication just before *La Rencontre au Foyer* had been painted, and already this small gouache contained a high degree of sophistication and courage of approach.
In his review of L'Exposition des Indépendants (Impressionist Exhibition) of 1881, Huysmans wrote about the two *aquarelles* that Forain showed: '... l'une, un couloir de

théâtre, peuple d'habits noirs, au milieu desquels s'avance dans une robe grenat une grande femme, et les hommes s'écartent ou la dévisagent tandis que le monsieur sur le bras duquel elle pose sa main gantée, incline vers elle le niais sourire habituel aux gens qui font des graces.' *L'Art Moderne*, (Paris, 1883), page 246. Allowing for a little artistic licence, this description may well apply to *La Recontre au Foyer*, for the second *aquarelle* was a *Loge d'Actrice*. Actually there was a third in the exhibition, which was a *Marine*.

By 1878 Forain had already developed a complicated system of cross-hatching. The slight hatching evident in this gouache, together with the form of signature, have led me to date it as 1877. This is a good example in which the brushwork has been applied so that parts of the woman's body are made more luminous, and others more weighty.

II FEMME DANS UN ATELIER

Oil on canvas; $10\frac{1}{2} \times 13\frac{1}{2}$ in. (26.6 × 34.3 cm); signed lower left *Forain Louis*; *circa* 1878.

Exhibited: Tate Gallery, London: 'The Pleydell-Bouverie Collection', 1954, No. 20.
Tate Gallery, London: 'Private Views', 1963, No. 155.
Roland, Browse and Delbanco, London: 'Forain', 1964, No. 9. Reproduced.

Provenance: Arthur Tooth and Sons, London/the Hon. Mrs Pleydell-Bouverie/Executors' sale Sothebys, 3 July 1968, Lot 4. Reproduced in colour.

Collection: The Hon. Mrs Pleydell-Bouverie, London.

In the possession of a private collector.

A delightful small canvas which is one of Forain's earliest, completely successful, attempts at painting in oils. He has kept to the same little size as in his gouaches, but whereas the latter follow mainly the same range of colour—varying tones of a palette almost entirely restricted to red, black, blue and brown, with pale greys and whites playing more of a part in the structure than in the decorative whole, *Femme dans un Atelier* is more realistic in its feeling for tonal values. The handling of the pigment has a nice freedom, considering Forain's inexperience in the medium, while the hatching, which would hardly be possible in oil paint, has been totally abandoned.

'Japanoiserie', which so delighted Whistler and made so deep an impression upon some of the greatest painters of the day, has evidently not left Forain untouched—hence the scroll upon the wall and the Japanese fan. The clear diagonal lines on which the composition is based are also an innovation for him.

III AU THÉÂTRE

Gouache; $18 \times 12\frac{1}{2}$ in. (45.7 × 31.7 cm); signed lower right *Louis Forain* and dated 1878.

Provenance: Mrs Laughton/Sothebys, 29 November 1967/Private collector, Rome/ Sothebys, 7 April 1976.

In a London collection.

Another theatre scene in the same range of delightful colour as the preceding gouaches on the same theme. Forain's awareness of the glamour with which artificial lighting could enhance a scene is nowhere better emphasised than in these small theatre and salon pictures. Here the *grande dame*, a particularly enchanting figure, is directly in the glare of the light; she is no down-at-heel lass unable to buy herself a drink, as in *Aux Folies Bergère* (Reid and Lefevre Gallery), but a pretty pampered thing in the full elegance of the Parisienne *cocotte* and perfectly aware of what she is about.

IV FEMME À SA TOILETTE

Oil on canvas; 25½ × 21½ in. (64.8 × 54.5 cm); signed lower right *forain*; *circa* 1884.

Exhibited: Eighth Impressionist Exhibition, at 1 rue Laffitte, 1886, No. 29. *Appartient à M. Durand-Ruel.* (Almost certainly this *Femme à sa Toilette*.)
Musée des Arts Decoratifs, 'Forain', 1913, No. 43. *Appartient à M. Leclanché.*
Roland, Browse and Delbanco, 'Forain', 1964, No. 2, reproduced. (As *Jeune Fille à sa Toilette*.)

Reproduced: *Revue Hebdomadaire*, 23 January 1913, 'Forain—Son Exposition aux Arts Decoratifs' by Louis Gillet, page 494.
L'Art et les Artistes, Numéro 21, November 1921, 'Forain' by Gustave Geoffroy, page 56.

Provenance: Durand-Ruel, Paris/M. Leclanché, Paris/Nunés et Fiquet, Paris/Julian Lousada, London.

Collections: M. Leclanché, Paris; Julian Lousada, London.

Present owner: Private collector, London.

Femme à sa Toilette is one of the few works illustrated by Louis Gillet in his very long review of the most important Forain exhibition held up to now.
M. Gillet wrote: 'La seconde Toilette' (there were two paintings of the same title exhibited) 'celle qui représente une jeune femme à mi-corps, accoudée, et qui, sous le rapport de la coloration, est peut-être la page la plus heureuse de l'auteur, est restée à l'état d'ébauche. L'artiste, par insouciance ou par découragement, peut-être par caprice, plante là, pour un moment, sa palette et son chevalet, sauf à y revenir plus tard; et, pendant quelques années, il ne fait plus que des dessins.'
I, too, think that this *Femme à sa Toilette* must be one of the most delightful, sensitive and tender canvases ever to emerge from Forain's studio, but I do not agree that it was left in its sketchy state because of *insouciance, découragement* or *caprice*. Forain struggled bitterly with many paintings which he was never able to bring to, what he thought, a successful conclusion. When one is so close to a work it is difficult to know when to stop; a picture is not necessarily finished when every part is carried as far as it is possible to go, but rather when the effect has been obtained and even though areas are still in a state of suggestion. It becomes alive when it takes over from its maker who, himself, may be surprised at the direction in which he is being led. In their happier moments artists accept this guidance; in their unhappier ones they ignore it and push on until they have killed their own creation. Today we have the tendency to prefer a certain sketchiness in painting, and so it is interesting to note that a critic of over sixty years ago was similarly attracted. But he still felt he had to justify his taste, hence his reservations about Forain's intentions.
Forain also thought *Femme à sa Toilette* was 'une des plus belles pages de ma vie', and tried to get the painting back from Mr Lousada in exchange for any other two canvases. The offer was refused.

V L'AUDITION

Oil on canvas; 20 × 24 in. (50.8 × 61 cm); unsigned; *circa* 1900.

Exhibited: Roland, Browse and Delbanco, London, 'Forain', 1964, No. 53.

Reproduced: *Arts*, Paris, 8 July 1964.

Provenance: Karl Loevenich, Germany/Mortimer Brand, New York/Arthur Tooth and Sons, London, 1955/Private collector.

In the possession of a private collector, London.

There is a small group of pictures in which Forain chose to mock at the cultural snobbery of Parisian salons where he had been a welcome guest since the middle eighties. It is said that, although he loved good food, he did not like those who made a profession of gastronomy for he hated affections of all kinds, and would-be intellectuals were not excluded.

In *Le Figaro* of 1902 two such canvases were reproduced: *Baudelaire chez les mufles* shows a young and fashionably dressed young woman, obviously reciting the work of that unique poet. Her appearance leads one to suppose that the author of *Fleurs du Mal* would be quite beyond her understanding, while the male dunderheads who comprise her audience are almost asleep on their legs. The second work is simply called *Dans le Monde*; the same young woman is again reciting, but now her eyes are turned heavenwards, as if she were deeply moved—not so the guests; they are either sniggering or 'nodding off'.

A third, *La Soirée Musicale* (W. E. Wallace/Sothebys 7 December 1966) is mainly monochromatic, as I believe the *Figaro* pictures to be, and this is what sets them apart from *L'Audition* with its colour pictorially enlivened by the generous use of Forain's favoured cherry-red. This canvas is splendidly balanced with beautifully drawn weight in the figures, especially the one on the right. It is interesting to note that Forain has avoided making a definite statement about the hands but the suggestions are so telling that the delineation is hardly missed.

The satire is less biting than in the 'Salon' series, in fact *L'Audition* might be categorised as an Intimiste painting had the story-telling aspect been lowered a little more.

VI L'ENTRE ACTE

Oil on canvas; 23¾ × 28¾ in. (60.4 × 73 cm); signed lower right *forain*; *circa* 1899.

Exhibited: Perhaps *Danseuses dans les rochers*, 'Exposition Forain', Bernheim-Jeune, Paris, 1909, No. 245.

Provenance: Hôtel Drouot, Paris, 23 March 1962/Reichenbach, Paris/Roland, Browse and Delbanco, London.

Present owners: Roland, Browse and Delbanco.

This is the best painting of *Danseuses sur la Scène* that I have seen, for the cartoonist has kept himself well in check and the work is narrative in the best sense, even though the actual situation is untrue. The simple rhythmic composition is based on two opposing curves; the weight, both in mass and colour, of the seated man is well balanced by the standing dancer with raised arms, while the light tutus again make a nice juxtaposition against the solidity of his black form.

Although the canvas is mainly monochromatic—this tendency in Forain's later pictures has already been mentioned—the warm brown undertones are sensitively relieved by glaze-like suggestions of blue-grey in the décor. The highlights are applied last of all to emphasise the flesh and the whiteness of the clothes.

VII AUDIENCE DE TRIBUNAL

Oil on canvas; 23¾ × 28¾ in. (60.3 × 73 cm); signed lower right *forain* and dated 1908.

Exhibited: Roland, Browse and Delbanco, London, 'Forain', 1964, No. 1. Reproduced.

Reproduced: *The New York Times* (International Edition), 23 June 1964.

Provenance: G. Salomon, Buenos Aires/Arthur Tooth and Sons, London, 1964/R. Shand Kydd, 1964/Arthur Tooth and Sons/E. Cartwright, 1966.

Now in the possession of the Lord Goodman, London.

This splendid court-room is about the most colourful I know. Although the tone is low it is enlivened by the cherry dress of the woman leaning forward, the orange in her hat and the red of the plume and epaulettes of the standing guard. The concentration of the three main *personnages* is beautifully caught. The tension is in the matter rather than in the execution, but this trait is general to Forain the painter—the difference between a *grand* and a *petit maître*.

VIII L'AVOCAT GÉNÉRAL

Oil on canvas; 25¾ × 32 in. (65.4 × 81.3 cm); signed lower left *forain* and dated 1911.

Exhibited: Galerie Raphaël Gérard, Paris, 'Forain', 1937, No. 45.
             Tate Gallery, 'The Pleydell-Bouverie Collection', 1954, No. 19.
             Roland, Browse and Delbanco, London, 'Forain', 1964, No. 52. Reproduced.

Reproduced: *Illustrated London News*, 6 June 1964.

Provenance: Chapelier Collection/Arthur Tooth and Sons, London, 1951/the Hon. Mrs
            Pleydell-Bouverie, 1951/Sothebys, Pleydell-Bouverie Executors' Sale, 3 July
            1968. Reproduced./Roland Browse and Delbanco.

Collections: S. Chapelier, Chatou-sur-Seine; the Hon. Mrs Pleydell-Bouverie, London.

Now in a London collection.

The quality of this painting is so fine that it could hang, not unhappily, next to a Frans Hals or a Daumier. Low-toned and generally monochromatic but for a few breaks into muted colour and a lovely use of whites and flesh tints, it is rich in its blacks and splendid in the handling of the shadows which emphasise the drawing.

I LA RENCONTRE AU FOYER *or* ENTRE-ACTE

1877. $13\frac{1}{2} \times 8\frac{1}{2}$ in.

11 FEMME DANS UN ATELIER

86

III AU THÉÂTRE

1878.   18 × 12½ in.

IV FEMME À SA TOILETTE

Circa 1884. $25\frac{1}{2} \times 21\frac{1}{2}$ in.

V L'AUDITION
Circa 1900.   20 × 24 in.

VI L'ENTRE ACTE
Circa 1899.   23¾ × 28¾ in.

VII AUDIENCE DE TRIBUNAL
1908. $23\frac{3}{4} \times 28\frac{3}{4}$ in.

VIII L'AVOCAT GÉNÉRAL
1911. $25\frac{3}{4} \times 32$ in.

MONOCHROME
PLATES

NOTES ON THE MONOCHROME PLATES

1 LE VIEUX MONSIEUR

Oil on board; $16\frac{1}{2} \times 11\frac{3}{4}$ in. (42×29.8 cm); signed lower left *Ls Forain*; *circa* 1876.

Exhibited: Roland, Browse and Delbanco, London, 'Forain', 1964, No. 23. Reproduced.

Reproduced: *Arts Review*, 25 July 1964; *Illustrated London News*, 6 June 1964; *Financial Times*, 23 June 1964.

Provenance: Chapelier Collection/Arthur Tooth and Sons, London, 1956/Mrs Peter Hughes, 1956.

Collection: Chapelier, Versailles.

In the possession of Mr and Mrs Peter Hughes, England.

I know of four other versions on this theme:

a. The earliest, and slightest, is *Le Galant*; pencil and watercolour; 12×9 in. Formerly in the collection of Mme Maurice Monestier, Paris, and now in the possession of an English private owner; *circa* 1876. The stiff figure with the knee muscles strongly held, is typical of both men and girls of this period, as is the form of the signature: *Ls Forain* (*see* Guérin, Etching No. 2, *Le Gommeux au Bouquet*).

b. *Le Protecteur dans les Coulisses*; pen, ink and gouache; $12\frac{1}{2} \times 9\frac{1}{2}$ in. signed *Louis Forain* lower right. Formerly in the collection of Mme Maurice Monestier, Paris; now in the possession of the Lord Goodman, London. *Circa* 1878.

c. *Le Dandy* is the only one of these five to be dated. Pencil and gouache heightened with white; $11\frac{1}{4} \times 8\frac{1}{4}$ in.; signed lower right *Louis Forain*, inscribed 'Gonnevilli'? and dated 27 fevrier 1878. Formerly in the possession of Anton Dolin and now in a private collection, England.

d. *Le Galant dans les Coulisses*; pen, ink and watercolour $11\frac{1}{2} \times 8\frac{1}{2}$ in.; signed lower right *jean louis forain*; *circa* 1879. After this date Forain very rarely used capital letters in his signature.

Le Vieux Monsieur always reminds me of two marvellous pictures which Degas painted of his friends between 1876 and 1877, and which I feel suggested the above series to Forain. *Carlo Pellegrini* (Tate Gallery) and *M. Halévy and M. Cavé on the Stage* (Louvre) are both wonderful examples of Degas' genius at revealing the personality of his 'sitters' through their mien. Pellegrini is witty, gay and lovable, full of amused dignity; M. Halévy, standing on l'Opéra stage and talking earnestly with his friend, is serious and deeply involved. Forain's fat little Monsieur is waiting rather pathetically to present his bouquet to his admired one. He knows he is no beauty and must compensate with rich suppers and presents, but in his way he is quite a lovable little fellow. As time went on Forain presented these suitors with more and more distaste and, unlike Degas who showed his individual friends, he painted a type whose story-telling aspect was of much importance. Only in this early series did Forain depict old and young rakes unaccompanied by the objects of their lust.

2 SCÈNE DE CAFÉ

Gouache; 12½ × 8 in. (31.7 × 20.3 cm); signed, inscribed and dated lower right *Forain/ à Seuri[?] bien cordialement/8 janvier 1878* (the year seems to have been added as an after-thought).

Collection: Frank L. Babbott, Brooklyn.

In the possession of the Brooklyn Museum, New York, presented by F. L. Babbott in 1920.

Had it not been for the actual date on this gouache, which confirms the method of its handling, one would have supposed it to have been prompted by Manet's famous *Bar aux Folies Bergère* of 1881 (Tate Gallery). As it is, Forain's minute painting was done three years earlier, although also around 1878, Manet used the effect of a mirror—but in much less complicated compositions, in other *Café Concerts* such as the one in the Walters Art Gallery, Baltimore. Since that time various painters have been intrigued by images reflected to and fro in mirrors and none more so than Degas' other disciple, Sickert. He so much enjoyed the mirrored interior of the Old Bedford Music Hall in London that it is often mystifying to separate the actual scene from its reflection or to work out the angles at which these mirrors were placed. *Scène de Café* is the only example I know of Forain's use of the looking-glass. Forain's great debt to Manet is without dispute and is especially visible in such areas as the play of light—Manet's usually daylight, Forain's, artificial—and in the rich contrast to be obtained by juxtaposing black against white and/or against flesh tones.

3 PORTRAIT DE J-K HUYSMANS

Pastel; 21¾ × 17½ in. (55.2 × 44.5 cm); signed and inscribed upper right *à mon ami Huysmans/ forain*; 1878.

Reproduced: *Revue de l'art ancien et moderne,* September 1929, p. 171.

Collection: M. Girard (the actor); bequeathed to him by Huysmans, 1907.

Present owner unknown—not in the Musée de Versailles as stated in the Bibliothèque Nationale catalogue, 1952, note to No. 13.

Forain made another portrait of Huysmans, an etching (Guérin, 61), which he did in 1909, two years after the writer's death. It is a touching and sad portrait bearing the deep marks of suffering the author had endured. Either it was etched from memory or from a sketch which, if it existed, seems now to have disappeared. Forain's homage to Huysmans; it was the painter's way of saying 'thank you' to the writer who had been the first to recognise his talent and to praise it in the press. He had also been, as Forain averred, the man who guided him back on to the path of Light. Forain was one of the founder members of the *Société des amis de J-K Huysmans.*
Photographs of Huysmans confirm that this pastel was a splendidly true likeness of the sitter with his fine head, clear-cut features and piercing eyes 'surveying visitors with a quizzical air' (Baldick, *The Life of J. K. Huysmans* (Oxford, 1955), page 60). He was thirty years old at the time.

4 L'AUDIENCE

Gouache; 10⅝ × 8¼ in. (27 × 21 cm); signed upper right *Louis Forain*; circa 1878.

Exhibited: Very possibly in the Galerie Raphaël Gérard exhibition, Paris, 1937, No. 86.

I do not know anything about this gouache but was tempted to reproduce it as it is in the direct line of Degas' *L'Orchestre de l'Opéra. Le Portrait de Désiré Dihau* (Plate xv) and before him of Daumier's *Le Mélodrame* (Plate xvi). Rather unexpectedly Degas has painted a group portrait, a nineteenth-century equivalent of a Hals group of burghers. Daumier's was an entirely sensational expression—dramatic and histrionic, in a canvas that has a wonderful sense of tension. While Forain, certainly showing an aspect of life of the Belle Epoque, has kept his narrative to a minimum, being mainly concerned with the play of dark and light shapes, silhouetting his two upright figures against the glare of the stage lights. *L'Audience*, in reproduction, gives the impression of being a full-size canvas whereas, in reality, it is a very small picture.

As it is the only work by Forain of this title that I know, I have suggested that it was *L'Audience* of the Raphaël-Gérard exhibition.

5 LA FEMME À L'EVENTAIL (Mlle Valentine H. Maria)

Oil on canvas; $20\frac{1}{2} \times 17$ in. (52×43.2 cm); signed lower centre-right *jean louis forain*; and dated 1879.

Exhibited: New York, Grand Central Art Galleries, 'Etchings, Lithographs, Drawings, Watercolours and Paintings by Jean-Louis Forain' from the collection of Albert H. Wiggin Esq., No. 269.
New York, Cultural Division of the French Embassy, 'Forain', from the collection of Albert H. Wiggin, 1950, No. 500.
Museum of Fine Arts, Springfield, Mass., 'Jean-Louis Forain', 1956, No. 28.

Collections: Charles Pacquemont; Albert H. Wiggin.

In the possession of the Boston Public Library, Albert H. Wiggin Collection, Print Department.

Forain painted several portraits of young women about this time, whose charming attire of the period seems to have attracted him every bit as much as their faces. Two of these are:
a. A tiny portrait ($8\frac{1}{2} \times 6\frac{1}{2}$ in.) of a young woman wearing a high fur collar in which her face nestles, and a hat with flowers at the back. She was evidently a Mlle Valentine H. Maria, for the painting is thus inscribed by Forain. She bears so strong a resemblance to *Femme à l'Eventail* that I feel certain that it was the same sitter. The portrait belongs to the National Gallery, Edinburgh, bequeathed by Sir Hugh Walpole.
b. Portrait of a plumpish young woman in a pork-pie hat and with a huge tailored bow at her neck; signed and dated *Louis Forain/18 Mars 1878*. Reproduced Geoffroy, 'Forain' (1921), page 54, and Kunstler, *Forain* (Paris, 1931), Plate 3.
Contrary to what is generally assumed, Forain painted quite a number of portraits; generally they were of his friends but also of young women whose looks appealed to him. Apart from self-portraits, his portraits of men were generally drawings or engravings.

6 UNE LOGE À L'OPÉRA (called 'George Moore leaving the Opera')

Gouache and oil on board; $12\frac{1}{2} \times 10\frac{1}{2}$ in. (31.7×26.8 cm); signed lower right *forain*; *circa* 1880.

Exhibited: Museum of Fine Arts, Boston, 'Painters of 19th Century Paris', 1935.
Fogg Art Museum, Cambridge, 'French Art of the 19th Century', 1942.
French Relief Society, New York, 'Forain', 1943.
Institute of Modern Art, Boston, 'France Forever', 1943.
Contemporary Arts Museum, Houston, 'Shadow and Substance', 1956.
Symphony Hall, Boston, 'French Painting', 1959.
Art Centre, Milwaukee, 'The Inner Circle', 1966.
Lincoln Laboratory, Lexington, Mass., 1972.

Reproduced: Jean C. Noel, *George Moore—L'homme et l'oeuvre*, (Paris, 1966).

Provenance: Kraushaar Galleries, New York/Mrs L. L. Coburn, 1923.

Now in the possession of the Fogg Art Museum, Harvard University, Cambridge, Mass., bequest of Annie S. Coburn, 1934.

Another delightful theatre interior which, although only slighter larger than *L'Audience* (Plate 4), also suggests, by the breadth and weight of its forms, a picture of considerably larger dimensions. Both are seen as 'close-ups', insisting upon a scale which admirably suited Forain. The semi-circular, vertical design of the composition is stressed by the white shapes of the shirt-fronts and collars and by the bow on the young woman's bonnet.

The Fogg Museum lists this painting as 'George Moore leaving the Opera' but I have no qualms denying it and the Museum itself has queried the attribution. The Metropolitan Museum, New York, owns a portrait of Moore by Manet of 1879, when he would have been twenty-seven years old; J. E. Blanche painted one in 1887 (Musée de Rouen) and Sickert a third, in 1891 (Tate Gallery). These portraits are all reconcilable even though the first shows Moore as a young man and with a beard. Forain's picture may surely be dated about 1880, just one year after Manet's, but his so-called Moore is no man in his twenties, neither does he have the long egg-shaped head and pronounced drooping moustache which lent the author so mournful a look.

Many years ago, the Fogg Museum was told, and by a descendant, that the '. . . gray haired gentleman in the box . . .' was Francisque Sarcey, famous music and drama critic on *Le Figaro* who wrote under the pseudonym of Santane Binet. This may or may not be, for we know how tempting it can be for historians and art dealers to try to identify sitters especially if they are well-known names.

7 L'ACROBATE *or* THE TIGHT-ROPE WALKER

Oil on canvas; $18\frac{1}{4} \times 15$ in. (46.2 × 38.1 cm); signed lower left *forain*; *circa* 1880.

Exhibited: Very probably *La Belle Acrobate*, Galerie Raphaël Gérard, Paris, 'Forain', 1937, No. 28.
Museum of Fine Arts, Springfield, Mass., 'Jean-Louis Forain', 1937, No. 28.

Collection: Mrs Emily Crane Chadbourne.

In the possession of the Art Institute of Chicago, Mrs Emily Crane Chadbourne Collection.

The excitement of the moment is suggested by the movement of the crowd rather than by the performer herself who looks comfortable enough to balance on the tight-rope all night. The illumination also adds to the drama, the lights spreading over the faces of the spectators, the tight-tope walker, especially accenting her balancing pole. This stress helps to hold the composition together for the mind's eye continues this line of light thus joining the performer with her audience in the lower half of the canvas.

In these early oil paintings Forain used little *allongés* strokes in the manner of Manet. He was still feeling his way with the medium and did not begin to feel at home in it before the middle eighties.

The tight-rope walker in her red-orange tutu shows brightly against the dark blue of the sky. Dashes of primary green and red emanate from the tent on the left, and a slight tinge of red is echoed on a face in the right foreground.

8 FEMME À L'EVENTAIL SUR UN CANAPÉ

Oil on paper mounted on canvas; 16 × 13⅜ in. (41 × 34 cm); unsigned; *circa* 1880.

Exhibited: Reichenbach, Paris, 'Forain', 1964, No. 7. Reproduced as *Intérieur*.

Provenance: Hôtel Drouot, Paris, 28 March 1962/Reichenbach, Paris/Roland, Browse and Delbanco, London, 1964/Capt. E. Bouskell-Wade, 1964.

Collection: Capt. E. Bouskell-Wade.

In the possession of the Ashmolean Museum, Oxford. Bequeathed by Capt. E. Bouskell-Wade.

The painting, besides the two titles above, was also known as *Femme sur une Chaise-longue·* It is one of Forain's rare unsigned pictures.
This charming painting has certainly not taken the sitter unawares. She is carefully posing as if looking straight into a camera, her fan suspended in mid-air and her left arm deliberately extended. Forain has again cursorily sketched in the hands as if he, like so many artists, had difficulty with them.
The intimacy of the scene is also unusual in Forain's *oeuvre*; he was not a natural *Intimiste* and after a few later essays within the family circle, he returned to themes outside his own home.

9 UN BAL À L'OPÉRA

Oil on panel; 12¼ × 15⅜ in. (31 × 39 cm); signed lower left *j. l. forain*; *circa* 1880.

Exhibited: Very possibly the *Coin de bal masqué à l'Opéra* in the Sixth Impressionist Exhibition of 1881, No. 21.
National Museum, Stockholm, 'La Douce France', 1964, No. 44.
Reichenbach, Paris, 'Forain', 1965, No. 5. Reproduced.
Kunstverein, Hamburg, 'Französische Impressionisten, Hommage à Durand-Ruel', 1970–71. Reproduced.

Provenance: Bellino sale, 21 May 1892/Durand-Ruel, Paris, 1927/Private collector, Paris.

In the possession of a private collector, Paris, since 1927.

As might be supposed from the theme, Forain, in this small panel, was able to indulge in black and white, the two colours which, on account of his main profession, were natural to him. Here and there the scheme is broken by touches of red.
As it is the only painting I have come across of a ball at the *Opéra*, I think it might well be the one, as suggested above, in the 1881 exhibition. Kunstler, *Forain,* (Plate 5), reproduced a *Bal masqué*, but this was evidently in a Café concert, whereas ours was evidently a grand occasion.

10 LE JARDIN DE PARIS

Oil on canvas; 16½ × 23½ in. (42 × 59.7 cm); signed lower left *j. l. forain*; *circa* 1882.

Exhibited: Roland, Browse and Delbanco, London, 'Forain', 1964, No. 26. Reproduced.

Provenance: Arthur Tooth and Sons, London/J. W. Freshfield Esq., London/K. Marr-Johnson, London/Arthur Tooth and Sons.

Collections: J. W. Freshfield, London; his nephew, K. Marr-Johnson, London.

In the possession of a private collector, London.

99

The 'Jardin de Paris' succeeded the 'Bal Musard' in 1881 as one of the favoured pleasure gardens of the Champs Elysées. M. Jean Lorrain described it as 'un éblouissement de chair et de soie sous les hauts feuillages illuminés à giorno, une atmosphère de fête galante' (Bibliothèque Nationale catalogue, page 35). These pleasure gardens flourished both in London and Paris in the last quarter of the nineteenth century; in London they attracted such artists as Whistler and his pupil Walter Greaves, both of whom painted in the Cremorne Gardens, Chelsea.

11 AU CAFÉ

Oil on panel; 9⅛ × 7⅜ in. (23 × 19 cm); signed lower left *forain*; *circa* 1883.

Exhibited: Museum of Fine Arts, Springfield, Mass., 'Jean-Louis Forain', 1956, No. 16.
Reproduced.

Reproduced: Geoffroy, page 52.
Kunstler, Plate 8.

Collection: M. Ernest Chapuis.

In the possession of Mrs H. Harris Jonas, U.S.A.

This café scene differs very much from the one already reproduced (Plate 2), for it was painted some five years later. The amusing marionette-like figures have given place to more realistic ones, especially the standing woman, who is seen in a different mood from the other visitors to the café. Their features are rather more exaggerated than lifelike and because of this the painting does not entirely hang together as a whole.

12 JEUNE FEMME SUR UN YACHT

Oil on panel; 18⅛ × 14¼ in. (46 × 35.9 cm); unsigned; *circa* 1883.

In the possession of the Sterling and Francine Clark Institute, Williamstown, Mass.

Though painted in a relatively low key like *Femme dans un Atelier* and *Femme à l'Eventail* (Plates II and 8), this attractive subject is, nevertheless, full of colour. The young woman is dressed in red with yellow gloves and she sits illuminated by the orange, yellow and blue lanterns. There is an explosive reddish light coming from the port in the background which seems to be *en fête*. A typically naughty Forain touch is the part-figure of the girl on the right, the curve of whose bottom echoes the shape of the lanterns and whose saucily placed feet re-introduce touches of red. The composition is intricate in its interplay of curves and right angles.
Most of Forain's young women wear a vacant, dispassionate stare, and this one is no exception.

13 AU JARDIN DE PARIS

Oil on canvas; 21⅝ × 17⅞ in. (55 × 45 cm); signed lower right *j. l. forain*; *circa* 1884.

Exhibited: Perhaps *Le Jardin de Paris, appartient à* Mme Langweill at the Musée des Arts Décoratifs, Paris, 'J. L. Forain', 1913, No. 42.

Provenance: Jos. Hessel, Paris/Bernheim-Jeune, Paris, 1918/Léon Orosdi, Paris, 1919.

Present owner unknown.

Apart from our Plate 10, there is a small panel called *Le Soir au Jardin de Paris* which was exhibited in the very interesting Forain exhibition at the Bibliothèque Nationale in 1952.

This is now in the Chapelier Collection, Versailles. Previously, the little panel had been shown in the Galerie Raphaël Gérard exhibition of 1937.

One imagines, however, that in the largest exhibition of his work ever to be held, that at the Musée des Arts Decoratifs, Forain would have wished to show his most important pictures and for that reason I feel that the above *Jardin* might have been the one chosen.

It probably resides now with some private owners in Paris—or elsewhere in France—who for many years have been notoriously private not only about the possessions they still have, but also about those they have sold. It makes the historian's task an extremely difficult one.

14 FEMME DEBOUT—Figure from *Au Jardin de Paris*

Pastel; $22\frac{1}{4} \times 15\frac{1}{2}$ in. (56.5 × 39.3 cm); signed lower middle left *forain*; *circa* 1884.

In the possession of the Toledo Museum of Art, Ohio. Gift of Edward Drummond Libbey, 1932.

Jacques-Emile Blanche ('Forain et Whistler', *La Renaissance Latine*, 1905, pages 412–13), talking about Forain just after Manet's death in 1883 says: 'La Gaieté de son atelier n'avait d'égale que celle de tous ses visiteurs. De charmantes études peintes, ou au pastel, étaient sur les chevalets, toutes entourées de feuilles de croquis au crayon, dont il se servait pour les bâtir, car il ne peignait jamais d'après nature et ne faisait poser que pour ses dessins.' It is easy to believe that Forain never painted from nature, for both he and Sickert had been taught to work from sketches in the tranquility of the studio; the practice handed on to them by Degas.

I cannot help wondering, however, what has happened to these numerous sketches as, to my knowledge, I have never seen a drawing directly related to a painting or even to any figure in a painting. I also wonder whether he squared his drawings with remarkable precision, as did both Degas and Sickert. I very much doubt it.

The *Femme debout* cannot be said to be a study for the finished picture as the figure itself is just about the same size as the whole canvas. One can only imagine that Forain—Pygmalion-like—fell in love with his own creation and developed the original small study into a large pastel.

15 LE BUFFET

Oil on canvas; $36\frac{3}{4} \times 58\frac{1}{4}$ in. (93.5 × 148 cm); signed lower left *jean louis forain*; 1883–4.

Exhibited: Paris Salon, 1884, No. 951; Musée des Arts Decoratifs, Paris, 'Cinquante ans de peinture français', 1925, No. 106; Galerie Raphaël Gérard, Paris, 'Forain', 1937, No. 27; Galerie Charpentier, Paris, 'Autour de 1900', 1950, No. 82; Bibliothèque Nationale, Paris, 'Forain', 1952, No. 159.

Reproduced: Geoffroy, page 53; Kunstler, Plates 10 and (detail) 12.

Collections: Jos. Hessel, Paris; S. Chapelier, Chatou-sur-Seine.

In the possession of the Chapelier Collection, Versailles.

Forain had now raised himself upon the social ladder and was mixing with the beau-monde. Having decided to submit a painting to the Salon he went the 'whole hog', chose what was for him a very large canvas so that it should not be overlooked in so huge an exhibition and, just in case anyone thought he could not manage it, carried the whole thing to a finish that he must have assumed to be academically acceptable.

16 LE VEUF

Canvas; $55\frac{1}{8} \times 39$ in. (140×99 cm); signed lower left *j. l. forain*; 1884-5.

Exhibited: Paris Salon, 1885, No. 993; Musée des Arts Decoratifs, Paris, 'Forain', 1913, No. 44, *appartient à* M. Moreau-Nélaton; Bibliothèque Nationale, Paris, 'Forain', 1952, No. 164; Reims, 1952.

Reproduced: Kunstler, Plate 9.

Provenance: Vente Bob Walter, 1894/ . . . M. Moreau-Nélaton.

Collections: Bob Walter; Moreau-Nélaton.

In the possession of the Musée du Louvre since 1933.

Had Forain seen the widower through the same eyes as the interior of the room, this could have been a first-rate picture. As it is, and something like *Au Café* (Plate 11), his vision has become divided and the canvas falls into two parts, or rather, moods. The widower is beautifully drawn, solid and firmly seated in his chair, but he has been carried so far that nothing is left to the imagination. On the other hand the open cupboard, filled with the departed one's intimate possessions, her hat-box and scattered articles of clothing, are of a delicious texture in tints of rose, blue and white. Above all they have been left as a suggestion whose poetry has not become dehydrated.

Whether one likes the painting or not, *Le Buffet* is consistent and in that sense only, it is the better work. Nevertheless Forain achieved his aim, for each canvas henceforth was accepted for the Salon by successive juries.

17 L'EFFET DE BRUME EN GARE

Oil on canvas; $17\frac{3}{4} \times 22$ in. (45.1×55.8 cm); unsigned; *circa* 1884.

Exhibited: Musée des Arts Decoratifs, Paris, 'Forain', 1913, No. 54, *appartient à* M. Pellet. Hirschl and Adler, New York, 'Forain', 1967, No. 12. Reproduced.

Collections: M. Pellet, Paris; Docteur Robin, Paris.

In the possession of Mr and Mrs Irving Moskovitz, New York.

In his 'Gare Saint-Lazare' series of 1876-77 Monet, following Turner's *Rain, Steam and Speed*, developed the discovery that there could be a poetic side to mechanisation; that there was an evanescent, if unexpected, beauty in a train approaching or departing from a station. Forain, lacking in this sense the imaginative gift of the Masters and ever willing to try walking in their steps, painted, as far as I know, only this one canvas on the theme. But his picture can in no sense be dismissed as merely a Monet pastiche for in it the main point of interest lies in the group of silhouetted figures waiting on the platform.

Dr Maurice Robin was a friend of Forain's and wrote an article on him in *Les Hommes du Jour* (date unknown).

18 L'ABANDONNÉE

Gouache and watercolour on paper laid on canvas; $22\frac{3}{4} \times 18$ in. (57.7×45.7 cm); signed lower right *forain*; *circa* 1884.

Provenance: Kornfeld and Klipstein (G. P. and M. E. (Exsteens) Sale), October–November 1960/Reid and Lefevre, London/Sothebys, December 1965/Reid and Lefevre/ Sir Antony and Lady Hornby.

Collections: M. Exsteens, Paris; Mr and Mrs Paul Mellon, Washington.

In the possession of Sir Antony and Lady Hornby, London.

This very sketchy painting has a rare, haunting quality that has attracted me whenever I have seen it over a period of years. It is Forain in a more romantic mood than one might have thought possible—so far removed from Forain the cartoonist.

Forain once said: 'La plus grande difficulté c'est de savoir quand l'oeuvre est terminée et l'instant ou il faut la laisser.' (Gimpel, *Journal d'un Collectionneur*, Paris, 1963, page 213.) In this painting, as in *Femme à sa Toilette* (Plate IV) he has stopped at just the right moment.

19 LE PÊCHEUR

Oil on canvas; 38 × 39 in. (96.5 × 99 cm); signed lower right *forain* and dated 1884.

Exhibited: Perhaps *La Pêche à la ligne, appartient à* M. Camentron, Musée des Arts Decoratifs, Paris, 'Forain', 1913, No. 25.
Arts Council, London, 'Country Life', 1952, No. 10. Reproduced.
Roland, Browse and Delbanco, London, 'The Renaissance of the Fish', 1953, No. 18.
Exeter Art Gallery, 'Contemporary Paintings from the Southampton Art Gallery', 1955, No. 31.
Russell-Cotes Art Gallery, Bournemouth, '19th Century French Painting', 1960, No. 20.
Roland, Browse and Delbanco, London, 'Forain', 1964, No. 41. Reproduced.
Wildenstein, London, 'Pictures from Southampton', 1970, No. 28. Reproduced.

Reproduced: *Illustrated London News,* 6 June 1964; *Burlington Magazine,* July 1964; as a Medici postcard, 1950.

Provenance: Dr Barnes/Chase Sale, New York, 1912/ . . . Durand-Ruel, New York, 1916/ Durand-Ruel, Paris, 1917/Mancini, 1918/ . . . Katia Granoff, Paris/ Southampton Art Gallery, 1936.

Collections: Dr Barnes; W. Chase, New York; M. Mancini.

In the possession of the Southampton Art Gallery, Chipperfield Bequest.

Forain had gradually gained sufficient confidence to work on canvases of a decent size although, to my knowledge, he never painted again an easel picture as large as *le Buffet*.
The conception and timbre of *Le Pêcheur* is so personal that one could not think of anyone else who might have painted it, for this endearing picture has the same kind of whimsical humour as *le Vieux Monsieur* (Plate 1) of eight years earlier. No wonder it has been in such demand for exhibitions where, from personal experience, I know it is always a favourite.

20 UNE PROMENEUSE AU BORD DE LA MER

Oil on panel; 9½ × 7½ in. (24.5 × 19 cm); signed lower left *j. l. forain*; 1880–3.

Collection: S. Chapelier, Chatou-sur-Seine.

In the possession of the Chapelier Collection, Versailles.

As Forain was so essentially a painter of the urban scene it is always surprising to come across a country, let alone a beach, scene. I think it very likely that he and his friend Alfred Stevens—a painter of seascapes seen from the shore—spent a holiday together on the coast, for the latter started on the same *Promeneuse* subject around 1880 and continued his series for a number of years. These dates tally with Forain's few pictures on the theme and this fact, together with the similarity of their results, seems to be more than coincidental. Two other *Plage* paintings by Forain are:

a. *Promenade sur la Plage*—oil on panel; $8\frac{3}{4} \times 6\frac{1}{4}$ in.; signed lower right *j. l. forain*; 1880-83. In the possession of the Sterling and Francine Clark Art Institute, Williamstown, Mass.

b. *Femme au bord de la Mer*—oil on canvas; $27 \times 14\frac{1}{4}$ in.; signed lower right *f.*; 1880-83; Exhibited Reichenbach, 1965, No. 13; Sothebys, 30 April 1969.

The Bibliothèque Nationale also showed, in their 1952 exhibition, a drawing of the series in coloured chalks; *Femme à l'Ombrelle, circa* 1882.

21 PORTRAIT OF VALÉRY ROUMY (ROUMI)-MONTMARTROISE

Pastel; $10\frac{1}{4} \times 11\frac{1}{4}$ in. (25.7×28.5 cm); unsigned; *circa* 1880-3.

Exhibited: Statens Museum for Kunst, Copenhagen, '19th and 20th Century French Drawings,' 1939, No. 43.
Statens Museum for Kunst, Copenhagen, 'Hommage à l'Art français—from Courbet to Soulages', 1967, No. 53. Reproduced.

Reproduced: O. Vinding, *Franske Streger* (Copenhagen, 1949). Colour reproduction on cover.
Erik Fischer og Jorgen Sthyr, *Seks arhundreder Europaeisk Tegnekunst* (Copenhagen, 1953), Plate IX.
Merete Bodelsen, 'Gauguin Studies', in *Burlington Magazine*, April 1967, Plate 63.
Merete Bodelsen, *Gauguin og Impressionisterne* (Copenhagen, 1968), page 196. Part of this book was translated in the *Burlington Magazine*, September 1970.

Provenance: Forain/Gauguin/given by him to Dr Sylvestre Saxtorph, 1884-85; bequeathed to his niece Mrs Ulrikke Pries, 1934/Ny Carlsberg Foundation, 1934 and given by them to present owners.

Collections: Gauguin; Dr Saxtorph; Mrs Pries; Ny Carlsberg Foundation.

In the possession of the Statens Museum for Kunst (Print Room), Copenhagen.

Mrs Bodelsen, in her intensive studies on Gauguin, has no hesitation in stating that this fine pastel sketch by Forain is of the same cabaret artist as Gauguin's medallion relief of a singing woman, seen full-face and which is dated 1880. On the back of the pastel is written— not in Forain's hand—'Valéry Roumy (Montmartroise) *c.* 1880. donné par F. au peintre Paul Gauguin'.

Personally I should have thought that this excellent character study would have been done nearer to 1884—when Gauguin took it with him to Denmark—than the date suggested on the back of the pastel. Forain's portraits of women, in his earlier years, are far more stylised, whereas this pastel is extremely sensitive.

22 FEMME SE REGARDANT AU MIROIR

Pastel; $21\frac{1}{2} \times 18$ in. (54.5×45.7 cm); unsigned; *circa* 1885.

Provenance: Lady Epstein, London/Obelisk Gallery, London/Roland, Browse and Delbanco, London, 1964/W. E. Wallace, England.

Collections: Lady Epstein; W. E. Wallace.

Now in the possession of the Hon. Mrs W. E. Wallace.

The triangular arrangement, here achieved in this single figure, is one of which Forain became very fond in his later groups of court-room figures. He was also attracted by the curious 'pork-pie' hat fashionable at the time and painted a few other heads of women wearing them. In this pastel he has amusingly placed 'his and hers' juxtaposed side by side— a typical Forain touch in what would otherwise be simply a charming period picture. As already remarked, Forain was inclined to leave hands in a tentative state—this right hand is another case in point.

23 LA PIANISTE *or* AU PIANO

Oil on panel; 10¾ × 12¾ in. (27.3 × 32.5 cm); signed upper right *j. l. forain*; *circa* 1885.

Exhibited: Hirschl and Adler, New York, 'Forain', 1967, No. 35 (from which exhibition
              the picture was stolen).

Provenance: Ader, Paris/Arthur Tooth and Sons, London, 1964/John D. Rockefeller 111,
              New York.

Collection: John D. Rockefeller 111.

Present owner unknown!

Forain, like Degas, loved and was knowledgeable about music, and although he poked fun at boring musical *soirées*, he painted this little panel with all the seriousness of Degas' *Le Père de Degas écoutant Pagans* or *Mlle Dihau au Piano* (both in the Louvre). But it is with Lautrec's *Mlle Dihau au Piano* (Museé d'Albi) that Forain's painting has the most *rapport*. The women playing the piano are, in both cases, placed in almost exactly the same positions and are seen from the same angle, but Lautrec's is facing left, and Forain has added the figure of a listener. In this way he has divided our attention and because we do not know which is the focal point, he has not completely solved the difficult problem of a composition *à deux*.

24 DANSEUSE AU FOULARD ROUGE

Oil on panel; 13¾ × 10½ in. (35 × 26.5 cm); signed lower right *forain*; *circa* 1890.

Collection: S. Chapelier, Chatou-sur-Seine.

In the possession of the Chapelier Collection, Versailles.

The disposition of light and shade, the lack of concession to any charm in the figure, the largeness and weight of form and the intimacy of the scene, recall some of Degas' magical little monotypes of the brothel. This series of dancers in their dressing-rooms is, as already stressed, by far the most successful of Forain's paintings of ballet dancers.

25 LA DAME DANS L'ÉCURIE

Watercolour and gouache; 11⅞ × 8 in. (32 × 23 cm); signed lower left *j. l. forain*; *circa* 1887.

Provenance: Hazlitt Gallery, London/the Lord Kinnaird, Scotland, 1964.

Collection: The Lord Kinnaird.

In the possession of the Lord Kinnaird, Scotland.

It would have been surprising if Forain, sometime or other, had not become intrigued by the horse. His friend, le Comte de Toulouse-Lautrec, was a well-known horse-fancier who, as we know from his son's painting, *Le Comte de Toulouse-Lautrec conduisant son Mail-Coach à Nice* (Musée du Petit Palais), drove four of his own spirited animals and was also an expert rider. Forain's neighbour, Princeteau, also a friend of the Lautrec family, was a recognised *animalier* chiefly famed for his horses, and then beyond all these came Degas with his intense interest in the race-course, purely on account of its pictorial possibilities. He was no gambler.

Forain did not do many paintings or drawings of horses and I believe *la Dame dans l'Ecurie* to be one of—if not the—earliest of the paintings. It would not take too much stretching of the imagination to suggest that it might even have been painted at the Comte's stables.

26 AUX COURSES *now known as* LES COURSES À LONGCHAMPS

Oil on canvas; 29 × 36½ in. (73.6 × 92.7 cm); signed lower right *j. l. forain*; *circa* 1891.

Exhibited: Wildenstein, New York, 'Degas' Racing World', 1968, No. 91. Reproduced.

Reproduced: Frantz, *Le Figaro Illustré* (February 1902), opp. page 20. Ragnar Hoppe, *Katalog over Thorsten Laurins Samling* (Stockholm, 1939), Plate 237.

Provenance: Tchoukine, 1900/Durand-Ruel, Paris, 1922/Durand-Ruel, New York, 1922/Halvorsen, 1922/ . . . Thorsten Laurins Sale, Stockholm, 1939/ . . .

Collections: Tchoukine; Halvorsen; Thorsten Laurins.

In the possession of Mr and Mrs Paul Mellon, Washington.

This painting, and those on the same theme which follow, represent a kind of 'aside' in Forain's *oeuvre*. The mind automatically recalls Degas' famous series of Race-Courses and one can be sure that Forain accompanied his friend and mentor on some occasions. But Forain was not equipped to paint the horse, any more than he was the ballet dancer. He had specialised in and studied neither, and whereas, in his own field, he was a wonderful draughtsman, he was of different calibre from the great Degas. Moreover, as he was primarily interested in the human aspect, it is on the *personnages* of the race-course that he has focused his attention.

Aux Courses is the most ambitious and most narrative of the four I reproduce, and one would not have been surprised if it, too, had been intended for the Salon. But, as always, it is beautifully composed, shows Forain's apt handling of crowds, and is, in its way, a *tour de force*. Like the other paintings on the theme, it is light in tone and colourful.

27 LE CHAMP DE COURSES

Gouache on canvas; 30½ × 44½ in. (77.5 × 113 cm); signed lower right *forain*; *circa* 1891.

Collection: Vollard.

In the possession of Mr and Mrs Paul Mellon, Washington.

Forain evidently planned this sizeable canvas as an oil painting then changed his mind and did it in gouache. It certainly has an immediacy lacking in *les Courses à Longchamps*, as if it had been done in 'one go' which, indeed, must have been the case. Forain obviously realised that he might have lost the freshness had he worked in oil paint, a medium which requires so many drying-out intervals before other workings can be applied.

It has been suggested that the race-course is Deauville.

28 LE BON TUYAU

Oil on panel; 10⅝ × 13⅞ in. (27 × 35 cm); signed lower left *forain*; *circa* 1891.

Exhibited: Galerie Charpentier, Paris, 'Chevaux et Cavaliers', 1948, No. 58. Wildenstein, New York, 'Degas' Racing World', 1968, No. 92. Reproduced.

Reproduced: Marguerite Rebatet, *Degas* (Paris, 1944), Plate 48 (as by Degas, under the title *Aux Courses—Deux Personnes Parlant à un Jockey* and unsigned).

Provenance: Kornfeld and Klipstein, Berne. Sale of 'Choix d'un collection privée'. Sammlungen G. P. und M. E., October–November 1960.

Collection: G. Pellet and M. Exsteens, Paris.

In the possession of Mr and Mrs Paul Mellon, Washington.

Nearly every artist has what might be called his 'canvas of natural size', that is to say that he is happier, and therefore more successful, with certain dimensions than others. This has nothing to do with scale, neither is it any disparagement. With splendid exceptions already illustrated, the pocket-size picture was the one for Forain in this first part of his painting career, and this delightful little sketch with its composition easily zig-zagging across the panel, its mass formed by the intriguers in the foreground and set against the spaces beyond, exactly captures the spirit which the artist intended.

One finds from time to time that when an artist, such as Forain, makes a habit of signing his pictures, an unsigned but genuine work may bear a false signature by way of being 'helped' —many Modigliani drawings have been treated in this way. Mme Rebatet, in 1944, reproduced the then-unsigned panel as being by Degas, but four years later when it was exhibited at the Galerie Charpentier, it was correctly acknowledged as a Forain. It is difficult to say when the signature was added, but it must have been before the painting entered the well-known collection of M. Pellet and M. Exsteens. In their sale catalogue of 1960 *le Bon Tuyau* is reproduced in colour and is signed.

29 CHAMP DE COURSES

Pastel; 28⅞ × 36⅜ in. (73.3 × 92.4 cm); signed lower right *forain*; *circa* 1891.

In the possession of Mrs Barry Ryan. On loan to the Metropolitan Museum, New York.

There is a lively movement in the mass of the crowd on the left of the picture, and what is unusual in this pastel is that Forain has made some use of the shadow which these people have cast on the ground. It may be observed that in these other *plein air* pictures, although quite a strong light is indicated, the race-goers, ghost-like, throw no shadows at all; neither do the numerous chairs in *Aux Courses* (Plate 26).

30 DANSEUSE DANS SA LOGE

Oil on panel; 11 × 13¾ in. (27.7 × 35 cm); signed lower right *j. l. forain*; *circa* 1890.

Provenance: Knoedler & Co., London/Robert Sterling Clark, 1919.

Collections: Sir George Drummond, Montreal; Robert Sterling Clark, Williamstown.

In the possession of the Sterling and Francine Clark Art Institute, Williamstown, Mass.

Whereas Forain had, from his earliest paintings, made much of the effects of artificial light, he had hitherto used them to illuminate faces rather than as compositional means. In this series he has become more sophisticated and has introduced chiaroscuro for its pictorial value.

31 L'ABONNÉ ET LA DANSEUSE

Gouache; 11⅞ × 15 in. (30 × 38 cm); unsigned; *circa* 1890.

Provenance: Jos. Hessel, Paris/Bernheim-Jeune and Co., Paris, 1918/Mancini, 1919.

Present owner unknown.

This little gouache is bubbling with gaiety, but one should not be so seduced by its mood as to overlook the brilliant drawing underlying the locked figures of the dancer and her portly admirer, nor the stabilising rôle played in the composition by the standing maid with a tray of refreshments. Once again, the *bonne* with a tray was an invention of Degas' who frequently used it in juxtaposition with a nude drying or washing herself—in any case, the static figure against the one in movement.

32 AUTOPORTRAIT ET LE MODÈLE

Oil on canvas; 21⅝ × 18⅛ in. (55 × 46 cm); signed upper right *f*; *circa* 1890.

Exhibited: Petit Palais, Geneva, 'De Renoir à Picasso'.

Provenance: Durand-Ruel, Paris/ ... Tronche, Paris/ ... Adler, Paris, sold 2 December 1965/Petit Palais, Geneva.

In the possession of the Petit Palais, Geneva.

There can be few artists who made more self-portraits than Forain—the greatest self-portraitist being, of course, Rembrandt. There are paintings, drawings and graphics done throughout his career, and there seem to be only two which show him wearing his ginger-red beard—these are therefore the earliest. Apart from the painting here reproduced, the other one with a beard is *Forain lithographe* (Plate iv); it is a lithograph of Forain drawing directly upon the stone.

All the other paintings known to me show a clean-shaven Forain; they are:
a. Bust, facing quarter right, a jar of brushes on extreme right, hair long. Hôtel Drouot-Bellier, 18 March 1964.
b. Bust, facing quarter right, shorter hair and frowning. Printed signature upper right, 31⅞ × 25½ in. Collection M. de Galéa.
c. Bust, facing quarter right, wearing 'butterfly' collar and bow-tie.
d. Bust, facing quarter right and wearing glasses.
e. Bust, facing quarter right, lock of hair falling across the eye, and wearing a very high collar and black tie. Very sketchy, 31⅝ × 25¼ in. Palais Galliera, Paris, sale 15 June 1965.
f. Portrait of 1898, in the Petit Palais.
g. Painter with palette standing before empty canvas, seated model and dog on floor. 28¾ × 23⅝ in.; *circa* 1903. Musée du Louvre.
h. Similar to Petit Palais portrait, 28¾ × 23⅝ in., dated 1906. Musée du Louvre.
i. Half length, facing quarter right and wearing glasses, *circa* 1920.
j. Bust, facing quarter left, 16 × 13 in., reproduced frontispiece Vaillat, *En Ecoutant Forain* (Paris, 1931), *circa* 1929—two years before Forain died.

There are two interesting sketches of Forain—one a self-portrait which belonged to Vuillard, the other drawn by Vuillard, both done at the same time in Forain's studio and identical in composition and detail. In the self-portrait, Forain is full-face, looking at himself in the mirror; in the Vuillard drawing (Mme Beres, Paris) he is in profile, looking at the easel upon which he is painting.

Apart from these there are numerous other self-portraits, both drawings and prints. Many portraits show Forain wearing the soft felt hat, 'like a Canadian ranger', which he affected in his later years, even indoors.

33 DANSEUSE RATTACHANT SON ·CHAUSSON

Oil on panel; $10\frac{1}{2} \times 8\frac{1}{4}$ in. (26.7 × 21 cm); signed lower right *j. l. forain* and inscribed 'à Emma . . . '?; *circa* 1890.

Exhibited: Carnegie Institute, Pittsburgh, '30th International Exhibition of Paintings', 1931, No. 168. Reproduced.
Galerie Raphaël Gérard, Paris, 'Forain', 1937, No. 47.
Tate Gallery, London, 'The Pleydell-Bouverie Collection', 1954. No. 21. Reproduced.
Roland, Browse and Delbanco, London, 'Forain', 1964, No. 7.
Portland Art Museum, Oregon, 'Recent Acquisitions by the Norton Simon, Inc. Museum of Art', 1968.
Princeton Art Museum, 'Selections from the Norton Simon, Inc. Museum of Art', 1972–73, No. 42. Reproduced.

Provenance: Sothebys, Pleydell-Bouverie Sale, 3 July 1968/Hahn, New York/Norton Simon, Inc. Museum of Art/Sotheby, Parke Bernet, 2 May 1973/Peter Matthews, London/Mrs F. L. Hellman, San Francisco.

Collections: S. Chapelier, Chatou-sur-Seine; the Hon. Mrs Pleydell-Bouverie, London; Norton Simon, Inc. Museum of Art.

In the possession of Mrs F. J. Hellman, San Francisco.

On 5 November 1904, Forain wrote to Bernheim-Jeune, his Paris dealers:

> Messieurs
>   Le petit tableau à huile sur panneau, représentant une danseuse aujoutant son chausson le pied sur une chaise, avec un homme en habit noir à sa gauche est faussement signé de mon nom. Au première vue j'ai pu m'y méprendre la danseuse ayant été calquée sur un dessin de moi.
>   Veuillez agréer . . .
>   forain

This letter is interesting in so far as it shows that by 1904 Forain had 'arrived' sufficiently for someone to have faked his signature and possibly traced one of his drawings. We know that he had been extremely successful and affluent for many years, but in the world of art dealing there is no higher compliment than to be considered worth faking.

To my knowledge I have never seen the painting to which this letter refers, although a *Danseuse Rattachant son Chausson* was a subject to which Forain returned several times; *see also* Plate 30.

34 AU PIANO

Oil on panel; $8\frac{1}{2} \times 10\frac{1}{2}$ in. (21.5 × 26.6 cm); *circa* 1890.

Exhibited: Arthur Tooth and Sons, 'Recent Acquisitions. VIII', 1953, No. 15.

Provenance: Flavion, Paris/Arthur Tooth and Sons, London, 1953/Mrs James Fell, 1953.

Collection: Mrs James Fell, Vancouver.

In the possession of Mrs James Fell.

This little panel is boldly composed in vertical and near-horizontal forms. It is handled with the freedom of certainty and broad brush strokes of juicy pigment. Again the chiaroscuro is of paramount importance, with the girl at the piano not *contre-jour*, but *contre-lumière*, with an enlarged sheet of music carefully arranged so as to silhouette her head and shoulders.

35 COLETTE ET PAUL MASSON

Sketch, probably gouache and charcoal; *circa* 1894.

In the possession of a French private collector.

I have no information at all regarding this touching and charming picture, but could not resist reproducing it for, apart from anything else, the sketch is a document of the greatest literary interest. The attribution of the sitters is beyond dispute—Colette's is verified by the lithograph, *Étude d'après nature* (Plate iii); Masson's, by Colette's own description of him, a prematurely aged man who invariably wore a black cloth suit: 'He was grey of feature, inconspicuous and unforgettable; his little beard was like dry hay, his laugh thin and grating, his glance that of a bad priest.' (Colette, *My Apprenticeships and Music-Hall Sidelights*, (Harmondsworth, 1957, pages 38–9).
Paul Masson, an ex-President of the Law Courts of Pondicherry, worked in the cataloguing section of the Bibliothèque Nationale. His few literary works were signed *Lemice-Térieux* 'on account of his delight—and his dangerous efficiency—in creating mysteries', also of his love of punning. He was a daily visitor to Colette in the rue Jacob flat, during her serious illness and her lonely and unhappy days of marriage. 'Without being gay himself, Paul Masson devoted himself to cheering me up. I think, seeing how very lonely and house-bound I was, he was sorry for me ... I think, too, that he was proud of being so easily able to make me laugh.' (Colette, *The Rainy Moon and Other Stories* (*The Kepi*) (Harmondsworth, 1975), page 182).

36 LE PETIT DÉSHABILLÉ

Oil on canvas; 16 × 12 in. (41 × 30 cm); signed lower left *forain*; *circa* 1896.

Exhibited: Reichenbach, Paris, 'Forain', 1964, No. 10.

Provenance: Reichenbach, Paris/Peter Ustinoff, Paris.

In the possession of Peter Ustinoff Esq., Paris.

By this time Forain had become very interested in the equilibrium of lights and masses, and from then on he was to paint less with colour than with light. This gentle study, less dramatic than the reproduction might lead one to suppose, is painted upon a brown-red underpaint whose warmth infuses the almost monochromatic canvas.
Forain did at least one other painting of this model, in which she is also *en déshabillé* but seated on a chest reading a letter. Unusual for Forain, she is not seen in a 'close-up' but is placed at some distance from the easel, taking her place in the composition as the apex of a triangle. This painting, which belonged to the well-known art dealer M. Henri Fiquet, is reproduced in Geoffroy, page 58, and appears to be the painting now in the collection of Mr and Mrs H. Snellenburg, U.S.A.

37 MADAME FORAIN PÊCHANT À LA LIGNE

Oil on canvas; 35 × 37 in. (88.9 × 94 cm); signed lower left *j. l. forain*; 1896.

Exhibited: Galerie d'art du Théâtre Pigalle, Paris, 1931–2.
Reichenbach, Paris, 'Forain', 1965, No. 4. Reproduced.
National Gallery of Art, Washington, 'French Paintings from the Mellon Bruce and Mellon Collections', March–May 1966, No. 128. Reproduced.

Provenance: Mme Forain/ ... Comte Doria/ ... Reichenbach, Paris, 1965/Arthur Tooth and Sons, London, 1965/Mr and Mrs Mellon, 1966.

Collections: Mme Forain; Comte Doria; Mr and Mrs Mellon.

In the possession of Mr and Mrs Paul Mellon, Washington.

The title of this lovely painting is in the nature of an aside. The fishing-rod in Mme Forain's hand is a subtle, but necessary, lead into the path on the left of the canvas which carries the eye up into the horizon and lineally links the figures to their background. Mme Forain certainly does not look as if she is clad for fishing, neither can one imagine the nurse holding the baby until she gets a 'catch'.

38 MADAME FORAIN AVEC SON FILS JEAN-LOUP SUR SES GENOUX

Oil on canvas; $25\frac{5}{8} \times 21\frac{1}{4}$ in. (65×54 cm); signed lower right f.; 1896.

Exhibited: Hirschl and Adler, New York, 'Forain', 1967, No. 13. Reproduced under title 'Mother and Child'.

One of a small group of paintings done at 1 bis, boulevard Gouvion-Saint-Cyr, to which address Forain and his wife moved shortly after the birth of their son.
A pencil drawing of the same title and date ($8\frac{3}{4} \times 6\frac{5}{8}$ in.) was exhibited at the Bibliothèque Nationale, 'Forain', 1952, No. 174, and belongs to Mme Jeanne Chagnaud-Forain, the artist's granddaughter.
These pictures are compositions prompted by an event and should not be regarded as portraits.

39 LE PETIT MARIN *or* LE PETIT MATELOT RÉVEILLANT SA MÈRE

Oil on canvas; $25\frac{5}{8} \times 21\frac{1}{4}$ in. (65×54 cm); signed lower right f.; 1898.

Exhibited: Reichenbach, 'Forain', 1964, No. 15. Reproduced.

Provenance: Christies sale, 1 December 1970; Sothebys sale, 6 December 1973.

Collection: M. de Galéa (in 1964).

Jean-Loup, now aged about three, also with his mother. These two domestic scenes at the Forain home in the boulevard Gouvion-Saint-Cyr are both low in tone, but whereas the earlier is generally monochromatic in shades of brown, this one is mainly in blues.
These pictures do not only represent a change in the painter's attitude; they also mark the general renunciation of the use of positive colour.

40 CHEZ VOLLARD

Oil on canvas; $21\frac{7}{8} \times 18\frac{1}{8}$ in. (55×46 cm); signed lower left f; *circa* 1900.

Exhibited: Reichenbach, 'Forain', 1964, No. 12. Reproduced.

Provenance: M. de Galéa, Paris/Reichenbach, Paris, 1964/Arthur Tooth and Sons, London, 1965/the Lord Kinnaird, 1965.

Collection: M. de Galéa.

In the possession of The Lord Kinnaird, Scotland.

In his satirical drawings, Forain frequently directed his barbs against the *marchands d'art*; perhaps he was one of those artists who, although they work through them, really regard dealers as a necessary evil, who exploit the struggling painter and hoodwink the trusting client. It seems, however, that he seldom painted the theme, and the canvas here reproduced makes no castigating comment. I do not know what authority there is for the title.

41 L'ENTR'ACTE

Oil on canvas; 23¾ × 28⅜ in. (59 × 72 cm); signed upper right *forain* and dated 1899.

Exhibited: Arts Club Exhibition of the Art Institute of Chicago, 1922.
                  Art Institute of Chicago, 'Century of Progress Exhibition', 1933 and 1934.

Reproduced: *Figaro Illustré*, No. 143, 1902, page 6.

Collections: Durand-Ruel; Mr and Mrs Martin A. Ryerson, U.S.A.

In the possession of the Art Institute of Chicago, Illinois.

By the early eighties Degas had finished painting an actual scene on the stage; after that his *danseuses*, whether set in a suggestive background of stage or classroom, were the material for his formal aims. Around 1900, Forain must have spent much time behind the scenes at the Opéra; he painted among others *Coulisses de l'Opéra*, reproduced on the cover of *le Figaro* mentioned above; another *Coulisses* reproduced on page 11 in the same number in which the ballet, as so frequently happened, was merely an adjunct to the opera; again in *Le Figaro*, the *Défilé de Vestales*; and *Coulisses de l'Opéra pendant la Représentation D'Aïda*, Collection Chapelier, reproduced Kunstler, op. cit., Plate 13. All these canvases are 'storytellers'—they vulgarise the dancers and, with one exception, hit hard at the men who exploit them.

42 LA PALISSADE *or* THE DISPOSSESSED

Oil on canvas; 30 × 26 in. (76.2 × 66 cm); signed lower right *forain*; *circa* 1902.

Collection: Rosenwald.

Present owner: The National Gallery of Art, Washington, Rosenwald Bequest.

Around the turn of the century there gradually crept into Forain's pictorial vision the certainty that, henceforth, it was Daumier who was to be his mentor, his guiding star. Since the middle nineties he, together with many other artists and amateurs, had realised the genius of this man, and during the ensuing years Forain had slowly, perhaps subconsciously, been digesting the impact that Daumier's work had made upon him.
La Palissade relates to the Daumier series of Washerwomen, particularly to *The Washerwoman* in the Louvre, behind whom there are also railings, buildings in the background and the steady movement to the left of the picture plane. This is the only painting I know in which the older man's imprint is visible in any subject other than Court scenes. It is easy to recognise that *La Palissade* was a transitional work, for there is a tightness in the drawing, a general sense of unease which all artists experience when, finding themselves to be in some sort of cul-de-sac, they decide to change their route. Quite naturally it takes some time to get into another stride.
There is an etching of the same subject called *Après la saisie*, with figures similarly disposed but more buildings showing in the background and less wooden fencing (Guérin, No. 35).

43 LE PEINTRE ET MODÈLE

Oil on canvas; 23⅝ × 28⅜ in. (60 × 72 cm); signed lower right *forain* and dated 1904.

Around this period Forain frequently tried his hand at the subject of the studio. As he grew older, he admittedly saw the world through an ever-growing pessimistic haze which his so-called 'return to religion' did little to alleviate. But the most despairing of all his series is that of the painter and model, with the artist usually looking so despondently tragic that one wonders why he does not commit suicide instead of wrestling against his *métier*. One cannot but admit that this is a very poor group, of which I reproduce one of the best I know. Forain's complex character puzzled even his friends—Adolphe Brisson wrote of him, in 1900, '. . . il m'a laissé la vision d'un homme maigre, herisse, au verbe acide, au regard mauvais . . .', but that immediately, he modified this impression: 'Vainement j'ai cherché dans son oeuil noir le rayon de ferocité que j'avais cru y discerner naguire: je n'y ai remarqué que la tristesse. Et il me semble que cette melancholie était temperée par une sorte de bonhomie souriante . . . Le regard est attentif, aigu, froidement observateur; la bouche est ironique mais non pas méchante. Il-y-a du gamin de Paris dans cette tête osseuse, dans ce corps agile et sec . . .' (Brisson, op. cit.).

44 DANSEUSES DANS LES COULISSES

Oil on canvas; 27½ × 21⅝ in. (69.8 × 55 cm); signed lower right *forain*; *circa* 1904.

Exhibited: Roland, Browse and Delbanco, London, 'Forain', 1964, No. 33.

Provenance: Leicester Galleries/City Art Gallery, Manchester, 1938.

In the possession of the City Art Gallery, Manchester.

Of all the paintings on the subject which I know, this has a certain nobility; it is also the only one which seriously shows the dancers awaiting their entrance without the lurking figure of the *protecteur*. Hence there are no innuendos. I believe that this picture, too, belongs to the transitional period which appears to have temporarily affected even Forain's well-tried themes.

45 SCÈNE DE TRIBUNAL

Oil on canvas; 24 × 29 in. (61 × 73.6 cm); signed lower right *forain*; *circa* 1904.

Provenance: Mme Cassin, Paris/M. Roselli, Paris/Arthur Tooth and Sons, London, 1953/ Mrs Hayward, Sydney, 1954.

Collection: Mrs E. W. Hayward, Sydney, N.S.W.—destroyed by fire.

Forain's first painting of a Law Court scene was reproduced in *Le Figaro Illustré* of 1902, op. cit., page 4, so one may assume that he started on this series somewhere around that year. The picture here reproduced gives the impression of being more assured than *L'Appel de la Cause* of *Le Figaro*, but it has the same rather stilted, parallel strokes in the *avocat's* gown and behind him on the left, which were unusual for Forain and which soon disappeared in the freedom of his brush as may be seen in the *Avocat* (Plate 47) dated 1907.

46 DANSEUSE ET FINANCIER

Oil on canvas; 28¾ × 23⅝ in. (73 × 60 cm); signed lower right *forain*; *circa* 1907.

In the possession of the Chapelier Collection, Versailles.

The feeling of stretch in the standing figure makes a good contrast against the slackened weight of the seated man as does the fluffiness of the tutu against his sombre evening suit. But Forain had now resorted to the use of 'higgledy-piggledy' brush-strokes as a formula for the painting of a ballet skirt, and in the Danseuse paintings these became progressively uncontrolled and meaningless. Equally, and on the socio-political side, he saw his 'villains' more and more as being of the Jewish persuasion.

47 L'AVOCAT

Oil on canvas; 21¼ × 25¾ in. (54 × 65.5 cm); signed lower right *forain* and dated 1907.

Exhibitions: National Gallery, London, 'Nineteenth Century French Paintings', 1942, No. 3.

Provenance: Mrs S. Kaye/Thos Agnew & Sons, London/National Gallery of Canada, 1952.

In the possession of the National Gallery of Canada, Ottawa.

A splendid study of arrested movement set against the static figures in the court-room and the wooden 'furniture'; fine drawing in the face of the *Avocat*.

48 LE PRÉTOIRE *or* SCÈNE DE PRÉTOIRE

Oil on canvas; 25⅝ × 32 in. (65 × 81 cm); signed lower right *forain* and dated 1908.

Exhibited: Musée des Arts Decoratifs, Paris, 'Exposition J. L. Forain', 1913, No. 27 (untitled).
Arthur Tooth and Sons, London, 'Forain', 1935, No. 17.

Reproduced: Geoffroy, page 74, as *Scène de Prétoire* and mistakenly dated 1906.
Kunstler, Plate 55, as *Scène de Prétoire* and mistakenly dated 1906.

Colour engraved by Larouche.

Provenance: The artist/Bernheim-Jeune, Paris, 1908, as *L'Avocat et l'Accuser*/Felix Doistau, Paris, 1909/Doistau sale, Petit, Paris, 1928. Reproduced/Jacques Rotil, Paris/ Arthur Tooth and Sons, London, 1935/Tate Gallery, 1935.

Collections: Félix Doistau, Paris; Jacques Rotil, Paris.

In the possession of the Tate Gallery, London.

It is nice when the history of painting may be traced back to source and very unusual with Forain, the records of whose work are extremely vague.
The picture is similar in composition and in details of theme to *L'Avocat Général* (Plate VIII) as is the general disposition of light. *Le Prétoire*, however, is more *mouvementé* and shows more evidence of the cartoonist.

49 FEMME AU CORSAGE ROUGE—Mme Forain

Oil on canvas; 25¼ × 20⅛ in. (64 × 51 cm); *circa* 1906.

Exhibited: Arthur Tooth and Sons, London, 'Forain', 1935.
Galerie Raphaël Gérard, Paris, 'Forain', 1937, No. 1.
Musée d'Albi, 'Toulouse Lautrec et ses Amis et ses Maîtres', 1951, No. 248.

Provenance: Kornfeld and Klipstein, Berne, sale of 'Choix d'une collection privée'.
Sammlungen G. P. und M. E. Sale October–November 1960, No. 28. Reproduced.

Collections: G. Pellet, Paris; M. Exsteens, Paris.

As Forain painted quite a number of women's portraits, both of models and friends, it is strange that, as far as I know, only three have been exactly identified as being of Mme Forain, an eminently paintable lady. Of these, one is a pastel sketch made before their marriage in 1891 (Plate ii); another a tiny panel sketch done in Venice in 1893 and belonging to Mme Chagnaud-Forain, the artist's granddaughter; the third is here reproduced.

50 LA FILLE-MÈRE *or* SCÈNE DE TRIBUNAL

Oil on canvas; 24 × 29 in. (61 × 73.7 cm); signed upper middle left *forain* and dated 1909.

Exhibited: Musée des Arts Decoratifs, Paris, 'Forain', 1913, No. 17, as *La Fille-Mère, appartient à* M. Beurdeley.
Roland, Browse and Delbanco, London, 'Forain', 1964, No. 5. Reproduced on catalogue cover.

Reproduced: *Illustrated London News,* 6 June 1964; *Country Life,* 25 June 1964.

Provenance: Alfred Beurdeley vente, Paris, 7 May 1920/Christies, A. S. Frere sale, 5 July 1963/Arthur Tooth and Sons, London/City Art Gallery, Bristol, 1963.

Collections: M. Beurdeley; A. S. Frere Esq.

In the possession of the City of Bristol Art Gallery and Museum.

To my mind *La Fille-Mère* is one of the most beautiful and poignant of all Forain's court-room paintings. Its noble, triangular composition is enhanced by the rhythmic and varied positions of the figures. His use of chiaroscuro in such pictures (Plates 30 and 34) having been of short duration, Forain soon returned, as here, to his method of highlighting the faces and hands of his *personnages,* together with the white areas of their clothing and sometimes their documents.
There is an etching, *La Fille Mère,* in the opposite sense and therefore made after the oil-painting (Guérin, No. 36); there is also another in the same sense (Guérin, No. 37). Forain evidently decided that it was better for the figures to face to the left and therefore engraved a fresh plate, which is not an unusual procedure for an artist. This question of direction is an intriguing one; it is a sense of feeling what looks right and what looks less comfortable—really a matter of eye perception.

51 LE RETOUR AU FOYER

Oil on canvas; 21½ × 25¾ in. (54.6 × 65.4 cm); signed lower right *forain* and dated 1922.

Exhibited: Perhaps *le Retour au Foyer,* Galerie Raphaël Gérard, Paris, 'Forain', 1937, No. 79.
Museum of Fine Arts, Springfield, Mass, 'Jean-Louis Forain', 1956, No. 27.

Collection: Albert H. Wiggin.

In the possession of the Boston Public Library, Albert H. Wiggin Collection, Print Department.

For some time after the First World War Forain was still paying tribute to those poor souls who had been driven from their homes with the few possessions they were able to carry. We know that he had difficulty in relating figures to a landscape background; he tried to do so in his Lourdes and Religious series, and this is but one of the reasons why they did not work. In *Le Retour au Foyer* the ruined village is like a backcloth, but nevertheless the drawing of the people is as telling as ever and Forain is still able to protest, by showing his sympathy for them, against those who have brought about such a situation.
At the age of seventy Forain the painter was finished, but the draughtsman was still very much alive.

52 LE CHARLESTON

Gouache; 19½ × 18½ in. (49.5 × 47 cm); signed lower right *forain* and dated 1925.

Provenance: J. W. Freshfield, 1925 (probably sold for the artist by Arthur Tooth and Sons, London/sold by Tooth to John L. Galleranes, 1932/ . . .

Collections: J. W. Freshfield, London; John L. Galleranes.

In the possession of a private collector, London.

The scene of the 'wild twenties' intrigued Forain as the gay life of Paris had done some fifty years before. Both were the aftermath of a bitter struggle, but now all elegance had flown and the suddenly emancipated woman was anything but a charming sight. Forain was a man of seventy-three and in bad health, and although living quietly at le Chesnay, he knew what was going on in the metropolis and, as always, was fascinated by it. He has brilliantly captured the noisy, smoky atmosphere of the night-club with its Eton-cropped and scantily clad women, no longer making secret assignations but blatantly sprawling in abandoned poses to stress their newly won freedom. Not a picture approaching Forain's finest achievements but a singularly lively and telling document of the time.

The gouache is a sketch for a larger oil painting (23⅝ × 29 in.) done in 1926 which is in the National Gallery, Washington, Chester Dale Collection.

I LE VIEUX MONSIEUR

Circa 1876. $16\frac{1}{2} \times 11\frac{3}{4}$ in.

2 *Opposite* SCÈNE DE CAFÉ
1878. $12\frac{1}{2} \times 8$ in.

3 *Above* PORTRAIT DE J-K HUYSMANS
1878. $21\frac{3}{4} \times 17\frac{1}{2}$ in.

4 *Opposite* L'AUDIENCE
Circa 1878. $10\frac{5}{8} \times 8\frac{1}{4}$ in.

5 *Above* LA FEMME À L'EVENTAIL (Mlle Valentine H. Maria)
1879. $20\frac{1}{2} \times 17$ in.

6 UNE LOGE À L'OPÉRA
Circa 1880. $12\frac{1}{2} \times 10\frac{1}{2}$ in.

7 L'ACROBATE *or* THE TIGHT-ROPE WALKER
Circa 1880.   18¼ × 15 in.

8 FEMME À L'EVENTAIL SUR UN CANAPÉ
Circa 1880.   16 × 13⅜ in.

9 UN BAL À L'OPÉRA
Circa 1880. $12\frac{1}{4} \times 15\frac{3}{8}$ in.

10 *Above* LE JARDIN DE PARIS
Circa 1882. $16\frac{1}{2} \times 23\frac{1}{2}$ in.

11 *Opposite* AU CAFÉ
Circa 1883. $9\frac{1}{8} \times 7\frac{1}{8}$ in.

12 *Opposite* JEUNE FEMME SUR UN YACHT
Circa 1883. $18\frac{1}{8} \times 14\frac{1}{4}$ in.

13 *Above* AU JARDIN DE PARIS
Circa 1884. $21\frac{5}{8} \times 17\frac{7}{8}$ in.

14 *Opposite* FEMME DEBOUT — figure from *Au Jardin de Paris*
Circa 1884. $22\frac{1}{4} \times 15\frac{1}{2}$ in.

15 *Above* LE BUFFET
1883-4. $36\frac{3}{4} \times 58\frac{1}{4}$ in.

16 LE VEUF

1884-5. $55\frac{1}{8} \times 39$ in.

17 L'EFFET DE BRUME EN GARE
Circa 1884. $17\frac{3}{4} \times 22$ in.

18 L'ABANDONNÉE
Circa 1884. $22\frac{3}{4} \times 18$ in.

19 LE PÊCHEUR
1884.   38 × 39 in.

20 *Opposite* UNE PROMENEUSE AU BORD DE LA MER
1880-3. $9\frac{1}{2} \times 7\frac{1}{2}$ in.

21 *Above* PORTRAIT OF VALÉRY ROUMY (ROUMI)-MONTMARTROISE
Circa 1880-3. $10\frac{1}{4} \times 11\frac{1}{4}$ in.

22 FEMME SE REGARDANT AU MIROIR
Circa 1885. $21\frac{1}{2} \times 18$ in.

23 LA PIANISTE *or* AU PIANO
Circa 1885. $10\frac{3}{4} \times 12\frac{3}{4}$ in.

24 DANSEUSE AU FOULARD ROUGE
Circa 1890. $13\frac{3}{4} \times 10\frac{1}{2}$ in.

25 LA DAME DANS L'ÉCURIE
Circa 1887. $11\frac{7}{8} \times 8$ in.

26 AUX COURSES *now known as* LES COURSES À LONGCHAMPS
Circa 1891.   29 × 36½ in.

27 LE CHAMP DE COURSES
Circa 1891. $30\frac{1}{2} \times 44\frac{1}{2}$ in.

28 LE BON TUYAU

Circa 1891. $10\frac{5}{8} \times 13\frac{7}{8}$ in.

29 CHAMP DE COURSES
Circa 1891. $28\frac{7}{8} \times 36\frac{3}{8}$ in.

30 DANSEUSE DANS SA LOGE
Circa 1890.   11 × 13¾ in.

31 L'ABONNÉ ET LA DANSEUSE
Circa 1890. $11\frac{7}{8} \times 15$ in.

32 AUTOPORTRAIT ET LE MODÈLE
Circa 1890.   21$\frac{5}{8}$ × 18$\frac{1}{8}$ in.

33 DANSEUSE RATTACHANT SON CHAUSSON
Circa 1890. $10\frac{1}{2} \times 8\frac{1}{4}$ in.

34 AU PIANO
Circa 1890. $8\frac{1}{2} \times 10\frac{1}{2}$ in.

35 COLETTE ET PAUL MASSON
Circa 1894.

36 *Opposite* LE PETIT DÉSHABILLÉ
Circa 1896.   16 × 12 in.

37 *Above* MADAME FORAIN PÊCHANT À LA LIGNE
1896.   35 × 37 in.

38 MADAME FORAIN AVEC SON FILS JEAN-LOUP SUR SES GENOUX
1896. $25\frac{5}{8} \times 21\frac{1}{4}$ in.

39 LE PETIT MARIN *or* LE PETIT MATELOT RÉVEILLANT SA MÈRE
1898. $25\frac{5}{8} \times 21\frac{1}{4}$ in.

40 CHEZ VOLLARD

Circa 1900. $21\frac{7}{8} \times 18\frac{1}{8}$ in.

41 L'ENTR'ACTE
1899. $23\frac{3}{4} \times 28\frac{3}{8}$ in.

42 LA PALISSADE *or* THE DISPOSSESSED
Circa 1902.   30 × 26 in.

43 LE PEINTRE ET MODÈLE
1904.   23⅝ × 28¾ in.

44 *Opposite* DANSEUSES DANS LES COULISSES
Circa 1904. $27\frac{1}{2} \times 21\frac{5}{8}$ in.

45 *Above* SCÈNE DE TRIBUNAL
Circa 1904. 24×29 in.

46 *Opposite* DANSEUSE ET FINANCIER
Circa 1907.   28¾ × 23⅝ in.

47 *Above* L'AVOCAT
1907.   21¼ × 25¾ in.

48 *Above* LE PRÉTOIRE *or* SCÈNE DE PRÉTOIRE
1908. $25\frac{5}{8} \times 32$ in.

49 *Opposite* FEMME AU CORSAGE ROUGE—Mme Forain
Circa 1906. $25\frac{1}{4} \times 20\frac{1}{8}$ in.

50 LA FILLE-MÈRE *or* SCÈNE DE TRIBUNAL
1909.   24 × 29 in.

51 LE RETOUR AU FOYER

1922. $21\frac{1}{2} \times 25\frac{3}{4}$ in.

52 LE CHARLESTON
1925. $19\frac{1}{2} \times 18\frac{1}{2}$ in.

COMPARATIVE
PLATES

ii Jean-Louis Forain
MLLE JEANNE BOSC
Pastel; signed and inscribed
'à Mlle Bosc'; *circa* 1890.

i Jean-Louis Forain (1852–1931)
MARTHE
Etching; 1876. (Guérin, 12.)
Unpublished frontispiece for the
first edition of Huysmans'
Marthe: Histoire d'une Fille.

iii *Opposite top* Jean-Louis Forain
COLETTE (WILLY)
Lithograph; 10 × 6 in. (25.4 × 15.2 cm); *circa* 1894. (Guérin, 55.)
Reproduced *Figaro Illustré*, 1902, 'J.-L. Forain', as 'Etude après nature'.

iv *Opposite bottom* Jean-Louis Forain
FORAIN LITHOGRAPHE
Lithograph; *circa* 1895. (Guérin, 25.)

v *Above* James Tissot (1836–1902)
TOO EARLY
Oil on canvas; 28 × 40 in. (71.4 × 101.6 cm); dated 1873.
Owned by the Guildhall Art Gallery, London.

vi *Opposite top* Giuseppe de Nittis (1846–1884)
JEUNE FEMME ASSISE AU BORD DU LAC
Watercolour; 11 × 9½ in. (27.9 × 24.1 cm); *circa* 1885.

vii *Opposite bottom* Paul Helleu (1859–1927)
FEMME ÉTENDUE SUR UNE BANQUETTE
Oil on canvas; 25⅝ × 31⅞ in. (65.1 × 81 cm); 1908.

viii *Above* Jean-Louis Forain
APRÈS DINER
Watercolour; 15¼ × 14 in. (38.7 × 35.6 cm); *circa* 1885.

ix *Opposite top* Giovanni Boldini (1842–1931)
DIEGO MARTELLI
Oil on canvas; $5\frac{1}{2} \times 7\frac{1}{8}$ in. (14 × 18.1 cm); *circa* 1867.

x *Opposite bottom* Giovanni Boldini
DEGAS
Drawing on canvas; $25\frac{5}{8} \times 18\frac{1}{8}$ in. (65.1 × 46.1 cm); *circa* 1880.

xi *Above* Edgar Degas (1834–1917)
DIEGO MARTELLI
Oil on canvas; $42\frac{3}{8} \times 39\frac{5}{8}$ in. (107.6 × 100 cm); 1879.
Owned by the National Gallery of Scotland, Edinburgh.

xii *Opposite top* Giovanni Boldini
PORTRAIT D'UNE FEMME
Oil on canvas; 15¾ × 9 in. (39.1 × 22.9 cm); *circa* 1882.
Collection: Valentine Abdy, Paris.

xiii *Opposite bottom* Théophile Steinlen (1859–1923)
LES PAUVRES GENS
Lithograph: 17¾ × 10⅝ in. (45.1 × 27 cm); *circa* 1915.
The caption reads: '. . . les prisons, est-ce que c'est chauffé ? . . . '.

xiv *Above* Théophile Steinlen
LE 14 JUILLET
Oil on canvas; 15 × 18⅛ in. (38.1 × 46.1 cm); 1895.
Owned by the Petit Palais, Geneva.

xv Edgar Degas
L'ORCHESTRE DE L'OPÉRA. LE PORTRAIT DE DÉSIRÉ DIHAU
Oil on canvas: $21\frac{1}{2} \times 18$ in. (54.6 × 45.8 cm); 1868–9.
Owned by the Musée du Louvre, Paris.

xvi Honoré Daumier (1808-1879)
LE MÉLODRAME
Oil on canvas; 38¾ × 35⅝ in. (98.4 × 90.5 cm); *circa* 1860.
Owned by the Neue Pinakothek, Munich.

xvii Edgar Degas

MLLE LALA AU CIRQUE FERNANDO

Pastel on paper; 24 × 18¾ in. (61 × 47.75 cm); 1879.

Owned by the Tate Gallery, London.

xviii Honoré Daumier

L'HOMME À LA CORDE

Oil on canvas; 44½ × 29 in. (113 × 73.7 cm); 1858–60.
Owned by the Museum of Fine Arts, Boston—Arthur G. Tompkins Fund.

xix *Opposite top* Théophile Steinlen
FORAIN
Charcoal; 6 × 6 in. (15.2 × 15.2 cm); *circa* 1911.

xx *Opposite bottom* Honoré Daumier
LE DÉFENSEUR
Pen, pencil and watercolour; $8\frac{1}{8}$ × 11 in. (20.7 × 28 cm)

xxi *Above* Jean-Louis Forain
AUTOPORTRAIT
Pencil and wash; *circa* 1910.

xxii *Above* Jean-Louis Forain
SOLDAT DANS UNE TRENCHE
Pen and wash; $8\frac{1}{2} \times 7\frac{1}{2}$ in. (21.6 × 19.1 cm); 1914.
Owned by the Cleveland Museum of Art, Ohio—Dudley P. Allen Fund.

xxiii *Opposite top* Jean-Louis Forain
RENOIR, 1905
Lithograph. (Guérin, 79.)

xxiv *Opposite bottom* Jean-Louis Forain
J. K. HUYSMANS—*Posthumous Portrait*
Etching; 1909. (Guérin, 61.)

xxv *Top* Jean-Louis Forain
L'ENFANT PRODIGUE
Etching; *circa* 1909. (Guérin, 46.)

xxvi *Above* Jean-Louis Forain
LA BORNE (VERDUN, 1916)
Charcoal.
Published *le Figaro*, 22 March 1916; owned by the Bibliothèque Nationale, Paris.

Index of Plates and Works cited in Text

Note: Plate numbers are indicated after title of work. Unless artist's name is given, all works are by Forain

General Index